Madame Alexander

Collector's Dolls Price Guide #25

Linda Crowsey

COLLECTOR BOOKS
A Division of Schroeder Publishing Co., Inc.

The current values in this book should be used only as a guide. They are not intended to set prices, which vary from one section of the country to another. Auction prices as well as dealer prices vary greatly and are affected by condition as well as demand. Neither the author nor the publisher assumes responsibility for any losses that might be incurred as a result of consulting this guide.

Cover design: Beth Summers
Book design: Marty Turner

Founder: Patricia R. Smith

Searching for a Publisher?

We are always looking for knowledgeable people considered to be experts within their fields. If you feel that there is a real need for a book on your collectible subject and have a large comprehensive collection, contact Collector Books.

COLLECTOR BOOKS
P. O. Box 3009
Paducah, Kentucky 42002–3009

w.w.w.collectorbooks.com.

Copyright © 2000 by Linda Crowsey

DEDICATION

Madame Alexander Collector's Dolls Price Guide #25 is dedicated to Marijo Wilson and the late Polle O'Leary. Marijo Wilson first introduced me to Madame Alexander dolls and encouraged me to purchase my first Madame Alexander doll for my daughter, Susan. I met Polle O'Leary in 1976 in Dallas. Polle was a dear lady who was a very wise guide in my early days of collecting.

— Madame Alexander Doll Club —
For membership information write to:

Madame Alexander Doll Club
(M.A.D.C.)
P. O. Box 330
Mundelein, IL 60060 – 0330

PHOTO CREDITS

A Century of Dolls, Inc., Gary Green, Ann McCurdy, Lahanta McIntyre, Chris McWilliams, Terri and Anna Queen, Kyle Ratcliff, Dwight and Patricia Smith, Helen Thomas, and Susan York.

My Twenty-Five Years of Collecting
Madame Alexander Dolls

1975 – 2000

The Madame Alexander Doll Company was formed in 1923 by Madame Beatrice Alexander and her husband, Phillip Behrman. Beatrice Alexander was born on March 9, 1895, in New York City. The first doll hospital in New York City was opened by her father, Maurice Alexander. He repaired dolls, and sold new dolls and fine porcelain pieces. Madame grew up seeing the joy that dolls brought to children. Madame's first dolls were made of cloth. Her very first doll is believed to be a Red Cross Nurse.

Linda Crowsey and Chris Law, California, in the Fifth Ave. Showroom of the Madame Alexander Doll Co., New York City.

Linda Crowsey at the entrance of the Alexander Doll Company factory.

The Madame Alexander Doll Company made exquisitely beautiful composition dolls in the 1930s and 1940s. Madame Alexander won Fashion Academy Gold Medals in 1951, 1952, 1953, and 1954 for the fashions on her dolls. She received numerous honors for achievements in the doll world and her philanthropies during her lifetime. Madame died in 1990, but she will always be remembered. Her legacy of beautiful dolls are cherished by collectors everywhere.

I am celebrating 25 years of collecting Madame Alexander dolls. I purchased my first Madame Alexander doll, 14" Renoir, for my daughter Susan's second Christmas. I was enchanted with the quality and beauty. Doll shows, friends, and books introduced me to the vintage dolls. Friends that I have made through dolls have become extended family. The search for Madame Alexander dolls is the connection that brings people together.

Herbert E. Brown, Chairman and CEO of the Alexander Doll Company, and the Alexander Doll Company continue the tradition Madame Beatrice Alexander began by making the most beautiful dolls in the world.

Madame Alexander and Susan Crowsey in 1987.

Price guides must be based upon values for a perfect doll since all collectors need accurate prices for insurance purposes. Insurance companies and postal services must have a way to determine the value of a damaged or stolen doll. Collectors must also have a way to appraise and insure their collection. A price guide, while not the final word, is a starting point to determine the value of a doll. The prices listed are for perfect dolls. Imperfect dolls will bring considerably less than an exceptional doll, which collectors call "tissue mint." Original boxes are important because the information on the box helps determine the age and manufacturer of the doll. The prices quoted are for dolls without their boxes prior to 1972. Prices for dolls from 1973 to present are for dolls with their original boxes. Prices of these dolls would be adjusted lower if they are missing their boxes. Boxes can be a fire hazard. It is possible to fold most boxes and store them inside a larger box and place the boxes in an airy dry room. Collectors will pay a higher price for a doll in its original box. Beware of storing dolls for a long time in their boxes — clothing, wigs, and vinyl can fade or change colors. Also, vinyl dolls tend to become greasy or sticky when stored in their boxes.

Perfect Dolls

❖ Complete outfit on correct doll
❖ Beautiful face color
❖ Clothes and doll in excellent condition
❖ Has all accessories, such as hats, etc.
❖ Clothes not laundered or ironed
❖ Hair in original set

Less Than Perfect Dolls

❖ Re-dressed or has part of original clothes
❖ Washed, cleaned, ironed clothes
❖ Stains, soil, faded, shelf dust, holes in fabric
❖ Faded face color
❖ Tag cut or missing
❖ Hair mussed or dirty

Exceptional Dolls

❖ Extremely rare doll
❖ Has wrist tag or original box
❖ Autographed by Madame Alexander
❖ Unique outfit or doll
❖ "Tissue Mint" condition
❖ Has wardrobe or trunk
❖ Matched set of same year (such as "Little Women")

There is no guarantee that any doll, antique or modern, will appreciate year after year. Prices remain high on exceptional dolls and always will.

Scarlett (left) is a mint doll in a very hard to find print. Scarlett (right) is a good doll and all original. The doll on the right would be valued at less than half of the mint doll because the dress has been laundered, hair mussed, and the condition is of a shelf-worn doll.

Mold Marks

Mold marks can be the same for an extended period of time. For example, 14" "Mary Ann" dolls will be marked "1965" which is the first year the doll was made. From then to now, all "Mary Ann" dolls will be marked "1965." Another example is the 21" "Jacqueline" first introduced in 1961. This doll has been used for the Portraits since 1965 and up to now still bears the 1961 date mark on head. Determining the exact year can be difficult for that reason.

Doll Names

The dolls named after real people are listed with last name first. (Example: "Bliss, Betty Taylor.") Make-believe doll names will be listed with first name first. (Example: "Tommy Snooks.")

Abbreviations

h.p. – hard plastic
compo. – composition
FAD – factory altered dress
SLNW – straight leg, non-walker
SLW – straight leg walker
BKW – bend knee walker
BK – bend knee
U.F.D.C. – United Federation of Doll
    Clubs
M.A.D.C. – Madame Alexander Doll
    Club
C.U. – Collectors United

Box Numbers

Order/box numbers for the 8" dolls with "0" prefix (example: 0742) were used in 1973 only. It must be noted the box numbers found with doll's name are from the Madame Alexander catalogs, but many dolls were placed in wrong boxes by the stores from which they were sold.

Auction Prices

Auction prices bear little or no effect on general pricing for Madame Alexander dolls. Recently, several dolls were sold at auction for exorbitant prices. It is as simple as two or more people wanting the same item — the bidders just get carried away! Another reason is the rarity or the pristine condition of a doll. This type of doll is extremely difficult to find and warrants the high auction price.

The final word is Madame Alexander dolls have always been collectible and should continue to be. They should endure in time and value. Wise collectors purchase dolls that they really like rather than purchasing dolls that are rumored to go up in value. Then, even if the doll's value doesn't go up, the collector has a beautiful doll that he or she loves. We hope you will continue to build the collections you desire, be they of older dolls or the wonderful current dolls that become available each year.

8" Alexanderkins, Wendy Ann, Wendy, or Wendykin

1953 – 1976	Has "Alex" on back of doll.
1953	First year of production, straight leg, non-walker. Only year Quizkins were produced with two buttons on their back for the head to nod yes or no.
1954	Straight leg walker.
1955	Straight leg walker with no painted lashes under the eye.
1956 – 1965	Bend knee walker.
1965 – 1972	Bend knee, does not walk.
1973 – 1976	Straight leg, non-walker with "Alex" on back of doll.
1977 – Present	Has "Alexander" on back.

The Many Faces
of
Madame Alexander Dolls

Wendy Ann (composition)

Tiny & Little Betty

Princess Elizabeth

Maggie

Margaret (O'Brien)

Cissy

ELISE (1950S – 1960S)

LISSY (1950S)

CISSETTE

MARY-BEL

JACQUELINE

MARY ANN

The Many Faces of Madame Alexander Dolls

ELISE (1960s – 1980s)

POLLY & LESLIE

NANCY DREW

WENDY ANN — NEW 1988 FACE

MAGGIE MIXUP (1960 – 1961)

WENDY ANN (1953 – 1965)

············· PLEASE READ "WHAT IS A PRICE GUIDE?" FOR ADDITIONAL INFORMATION ···················

ACTIVE MISS — 18" h.p., 1954 only (Violet/Cissy) 850.00
ADAMS, ABIGAIL — 1976–1978, Presidents' Ladies/First Ladies Series, First Set (Mary Ann) 125.00
ADAMS, LOUISA — 1976–1978, Presidents' Ladies/First Ladies Series, First Set (Louisa) 125.00
ADDAMS FAMILY — #31130, 1997 – 1998, set 4 dolls (8", 10") and Thing. 350.00
    #31110, 1997 – 1998, 10" Gomez and Morticia 180.00
    #31120, 1997 – 1998, 8" Wednesday and Pugsley 160.00
AFRICA — 8" h.p., #766, 1966–1971, BK (Wendy Ann) 265.00
    8" h.p. straight leg, re-issued, #523–583, 1988–1992 (Wendy Ann) 60.00
AGATHA — 18" h.p. (Cissy)
    1954 only, Me and My Shadow Series, rose taffeta dress, excellent face color 1,850.00
    8" h.p. (Wendy Ann), #00308, 1953–1954, black top and floral gown . . . . 1,300.00 up
    21" Portrait, #2171, 1967, red gown (Jacqueline) 675.00
        #2297, 1974, rose gown with full length cape (Jacqueline) 475.00
        #2291, 1975, blue with white sequin trim (Jacqueline) 375.00
        #2294, 1976, blue with white rick-rack trim (Jacqueline). 350.00
        #2230, 1979, 1980, lavender. 275.00
        #2230, 1981, turquoise blue (Jacqueline) 275.00
    10" Portrette, #1171, 1968 only, red velvet (Cissette). 450.00
AGNES — Cloth/felt, 1930s. 750.00
ALADDIN — 8" h.p., #482, 1993; #140482, 1994 only, Storybook Series 60.00
ALASKA — 8", #302, 1990–1992, Americana Series (Maggie smile face). 55.00
ALBANIA — 8" straight leg, #526, 1987 only (Wendy Ann). 60.00
ALCOTT, LOUISA MAY — 14", #1529, 1989–1990, Classic Series (Mary Ann) 85.00
    8" h.p., #409, 1992 only, Storyland Series (Wendy Ann). 75.00
ALEGRIA — 10", h.p., #20118, 1996 Cirque du Soleil, silver outfit 95.00
ALEXANDER RAG TIME DOLLS — Cloth, 1938–1939 only. . . . . 850.00 up
ALEXANDER-KINS — 7½–8" h.p., must have excellent face color
(Also referred to as **WENDY, WENDY ANN**, or **WENDY-KIN**.) *If doll is not listed here, see regular listing for name.*
(Add more for mint or mint in box dolls. Special hairdos are higher priced.)
    Straight leg non-walker, 1953 (Add more for Quiz-Kins)
        Coat/hat (dress). 550.00
        Cotton dress/organdy or cotton pinafore/hat. 525.00
        Dresser/doll/wardrobe, mint . . . . 3,200.00 up
        Easter doll . . . . 925.00 up
        Felt jackets/pleated skirt dresses 525.00
        Garden Party long gown. . . . . 1,300.00 up
        Jumper/one-piece bodysuit 375.00
        Nightgown. 275.00
        Nude/perfect doll (excellent face color) 225.00
        Organdy dress/cotton or organdy pinafore/hat 550.00
        Satin dress/organdy or cotton pinafore/hat. 650.00
        Sleeveless satin dress/organdy or cotton pinafore 475.00
        Taffeta dress/cotton pinafore/hat 650.00
        Robe/nightgown or P.J.'s. 300.00
    Straight leg walker, 1954–1955, must have good face color. (Add more for mint or mint in box dolls.)
        Basic doll in box/panties/shoes/socks. 400.00
        Coat/hat (dress) . . . . 425.00 up
        Cotton dress/pinafore/hat . . . . 425.00 up
        Cotton school dress. 325.00
        Day in Country 875.00
        Garden Party long gown. . . . . 1,300.00 up
        Maypole Dance 550.00

Nightgown, robe, or PJs 225.00
Jumper dress with blouse effect, any material. 350.00
Organdy party dress/hat . . . . 450.00 up
Riding Habit. . . . . 375.00 up
Sailor dress . . . . 875.00 up
Sleeveless organdy dress 350.00
Swimsuits (mint). 325.00
Taffeta/satin party dress/hat . . . . 500.00 up
Bend knee walker, 1956–1965, must have good face color. (Add more for mint or mint in box dolls.)
"Alexander-kin" dropped in 1963 and "Wendy Ann" used through 1965
Nude (Excellent face color) 125.00
Basic doll in box/panties/shoes/socks (mint in box) 375.00
Carcoat set. 850.00
Cherry Twin . . . . Each – 1,500.00 up
Coat/hat/dress. 375.00
Cotton dress/cotton pinafore/hat 375.00
Cotton or satin dress/organdy pinafore/hat . . . . 400.00 up
Easter Egg/doll, 1965, 1966 only . . . . 1,500.00 up
Felt jacket/pleated skirt/dress/cap or hat. . . . . 375.00 up
First Dancing Dress (gown). 750.00
Flowergirl. . . . . 850.00 up
French braid/cotton dress, 1965. . . . . 575.00
June Wedding 750.00
Long party dress . . . . 800.00 up
Nightgown/robe 225.00
NEIMAN-MARCUS (clothes must be on correct doll with correct hairdo)
Doll in case with all clothes. . . . . 1,350.00 up
Name of store printed on dress material 750.00
2 pc. playsuit, navy with red trim 475.00
Robe, navy. 325.00
Nude, perfect doll with excellent face color, bend knee/non-walker. 85.00
Organdy dress/hat, 1965. . . . . 425.00
Organdy dress/organdy pinafore/hat. 425.00

Alexander-Kin, 8", #468, 1955 (Wendy). straight leg walker. Plaid dress with felt jacket and cap.

Wendy-Kin, 8", BKW (Wendy), pink cotton dress. Tagged: "Wendy-Kin."

A

Riding habit, boy or girl 475.00
    Devon Horse Show 725.00
Riding habit, check pants, girl, 1965, boy 1965 . . . . 375.00
Sewing Kit/doll, 1965, 1966 only . . . . 950.00 up
Skater 575.00
Sundress 350.00
Swimsuits, beach outfits 325.00
Taffeta party dress/hat 475.00
Tennis 425.00

ALGERIA — 8", straight leg, #528, 1987–1988 only (Maggie) 55.00

ALICE — 18" h.p., 1951 only, saran wig to waist (Maggie) 750.00

ALICE AND HER PARTY KIT — 1965 only, included case, wardrobe and wigs, mint (Mary Ann) 750.00

ALICE (IN WONDERLAND) —

16" cloth, 1930 flat face, eyes painted to side 875.00
1933 formed mask face 675.00
7" compo., 1930s (Tiny Betty) 395.00
9" compo., 1930s (Little Betty) 375.00
11–14" compo., 1936–1940 (Wendy Ann) 400.00–450.00
13" compo., 1930s, has swivel waist (Wendy Ann) 425.00
14½–18" compo., 1948–1949 (Margaret) 475.00–750.00
21" compo., 1948–1949 (Margaret, Wendy Ann) 950.00
14" h.p., 1950 (Maggie) 675.00
17–23" h.p. 1949–1950 (Maggie & Margaret) . . . . 625.00–800.00 up
15", 18", 23" h.p., 1951–1952 (Maggie & Margaret) . . . . 450.00–800.00 up
14" h.p. with trousseau, 1951–1952 (Maggie) . . . . 1,600.00 up
15" h.p., 1951–1952 (Maggie & Margaret) 575.00
17" h.p., 1949–1950 (Maggie & Margaret) 625.00
23" h.p., 1942–1952 (Maggie & Margaret) . . . . 875.00 up
29" cloth/vinyl, 1952 (Barbara Jane) . . . . 700.00 up
8" h.p., #465–#590, 1955–1956 (Wendy Ann) . . . . 775.00 up
8", #494, Storyland Series, blue/white eyelet pinafore 1990–1992 . . . . 70.00
    #492, 1993, #140492, 1994 blue/white with red trim 70.00
    8" h.p., 1972–1976, Disney crest colors (Disneyland, Disney World) 450.00

Alexander-Kin, 8" (Wendy) #586, 1956. Organdy and lace dress with straw hat with lace. Tagged: "Alexander-Kins."

Alexander-Kin, 8", 1954, straight leg walker (Wendy), pink taffeta jumper and hat.

8" h.p., blue with lace trim, organdy pinafore, 1995 ....70.00
8" h.p. #13000, 1997 – 1998, Alice with calendar,
   blue party dress, gold crown #13001–1999 ....75.00
12", Prom Party set, 1963 (Lissy) 950.00
14" plastic/vinyl, #1452 to 1974, #1552, 1966–1992,
   Literature & Classic Series (Mary Ann) 100.00
14" plastic/vinyl, #87001, 1996 Storyland Friends 110.00
10", 1991, with white rabbit
   (see Disney under Special Events/Exclusives)
18", #16001, 1996 Rag Doll Series (cloth doll)Not available for sale
ALL STAR — 8" h.p., #346–346-1, Americana Series,
   1993 white or black, 1994 white only 70.00
ALLISON — 18" cloth/vinyl, 1990–1991 ....110.00
ALPINE BOY AND GIRL — 1992
   (see Christmas Shoppe under Special Events/Exclusives)
ALTAR BOY — 8" h.p., #311, 1991 only,
   Americana Series 70.00
AMANDA — 8" h.p., #489, 1961 only, Americana Series, burnt
   orange/lace trim (Wendy Ann) ....2,000.00 up
AMERICAN BABIES — 16–18" cloth, 1930s 175.00–350.00
AMERICAN BEAUTY — 10" Portrette, #1142,
   1991–1992, all pink 90.00
AMERICAN FARM COUPLE — 8", 1997, #22160,
   1930s rural America 130.00
AMERICAN GIRL — 7–8" compo., 1938 (Tiny Betty) 385.00
   9–11" compo., 1937 (Little Betty, Wendy Ann) ...350.00–450.00
   8" h.p., #388, #788, 1962–1963, became "McGuffey Ana"
      in 1964–1965 (Wendy Ann) 375.00
AMERICAN INDIAN — 9" compo., 1938–1939 (Little Betty) 350.00
AMERICAN LEGEND, AN — 10", #12510, 1999,
   with hardcover book 250.00

Alexander-Kin, 8", #539, 1956, BKW (Wendy). A very special hairdo with a curl pulled to the back. Outfit has a special slip of navy blue trimmed in rick-rack. Tagged: "Alexander-Kins."

AMERICAN TOTS — 16–21" cloth, dressed in child's fashions..........................275.00–500.00
AMERICAN WOMEN'S VOLUNTEER SERVICE (A.W.V.S.) — 14" compo., 1942 (Wendy Ann)...............825.00 up
AMISH BOY — 8" h.p., BK, #727, 1966–1969, Americana Series (Wendy Ann).......................375.00
AMISH GIRL — 8" h.p. BK, #726, 1966–1969, Americana Series (Wendy Ann).......................375.00
AMY — (see Little Women)
AMY GOES TO PARIS TRUNK SET — 8", #14635, 1996...200.00
AMY THE BRIDE — 10", #14622, 1996, ivory lace dress..100.00
ANASTASIA — 10" Portrette, #1125, 1988–1989 (Cissette)..90.00
   14" (see M.A.D.C. under Special Events/Exclusives)
ANATOLIA — 8", straight leg, #524, 1987 only...65.00
ANGEL AND 8" MUSIC BOX CRECHE — 8", #19530, 1997–1999, Nativity set..........................250.00
ANGEL — 8", in pink, blue, off-white gowns (Wendy & Maggie)..................................900.00 up
   BABY ANGEL — 8" h.p. #480, 1955, multi-layered chiffon wings (Wendy Ann)..................950.00 up
   GUARDIAN ANGEL — 8", #480, 1954 only (Wendy Ann)...825.00 up
   GUARDIAN ANGEL — 8", #618, 1961 (Maggie smile face)......................................750.00
   GUARDIAN ANGEL — 10", #10602, 1995, first in series, all pink with white wings............110.00
   PRISTINE ANGEL — 10", #10604, 1995, second in series, white with gold trim................110.00
ANGEL FACE — (see Shirley's Doll House under Special Events/Exclusives)
ANGEL TREE TOPPER — (see Tree Topper)
ANN ESTELLE — 8", #17600, 1999, Mary Engelbreit sailor outfit...............................70.00
ANNA AND THE KING OF SIAM — 8", 1996, #14656, sold as set..................................160.00
ANNA BALLERINA — 18" compo., 1940, Pavlova (Wendy Ann).....................................950.00 up
ANNABELLE — 14–15" h.p., 1951–1952 only, Kate Smith's stories of Annabelle (Maggie).........575.00
   14–15" trousseau/trunk, 1952 only, FAO Schwarz (Maggie)...................................1,500.00 up
   18" h.p., 1951–1952 (Maggie)...700.00
   20–23" h.p., 1951–1952 (Maggie)...700.00–875.00 up
ANNABELLE AT CHRISTMAS — (see Belks & Leggett under Special Events/Exclusives)

ANNA KARENINA — 21" Portrait, #2265, 1991 (Jacqueline) 350.00
    10", #21900, (Cissette) bustle dress, 1998–1999... 125.00
    10", #21910, (Cissette) Trunk set, doll, 3 outfits, 1998–1999............................. 275.00
ANNE OF GREEN GABLES — 14", #1530, 1989–1990 only (Mary Ann) 125.00
    14", #1579, 1992–1994, Goes to School, with trunk/wardrobe (Louisa/Jennifer)................. 225.00
    14", #1570 in 1993 only, #261501 in 1995, Arrives at Station.............................. 150.00
    14", 1993, Becomes the Teacher 125.00
    8" h.p. 1994–1995, #260417, At the Station (Wendy Ann) 85.00
    8" h.p. 1994, #260418 puff sleeve dress 95.00
    8" h.p., #26423, 1995, concert dress 85.00
    8" h.p., #26421, 1995, trunk playset 200.00
    8" h.p., #13830, 1998–1999, floral dress, drawstring bag, straw hat 80.00
ANNETTE — 1993 (see Disney under Special Events/Exclusives)
ANNIE THE ARTIST — 20", #35001, 1996, artist outfit, crayons .... Not available for sale
ANNIE LAURIE — 14" compo., 1937 (Wendy Ann)... 650.00
    17" compo., 1937 (Wendy Ann) 925.00
ANTOINETTE — 21" compo., 1946, extra makeup, must be mint (Wendy Ann)............... 2,100.00 up
ANTOINETTE, MARIE — 21", 1987–1988 only, multi-floral with pink front insert 375.00
ANTONY, MARK — 12", #1310, 1980–1985, Portraits of History (Nancy Drew) 65.00
APPLE ANNIE OF BROADWAY — 8" h.p., 1953–1954 (Wendy Ann) .... 1,000.00 up
APPLE PIE — 14", #1542, 1991 only, Doll Classics (Mary Ann) 95.00
APPLE TREE — 8", #13290, 1999, dressed as a tree trunk with leaves and apples 76.00
APRIL — 14", #1533, 1990–1991, Doll Classics (Mary Ann & Jennifer)......................... 95.00
APRIL SHOWERS BRING MAY FLOWERS — 8", #13480, 1998–1999, pink taffeta and lace, parasol 100.00
AQUARIUS — 8", #21310, 1998, orange and gold mermaid costume 90.00
ARGENTINE BOY — 8" h.p., BKW & BK, #772, 1965 only (Wendy Ann) 525.00
ARGENTINE GIRL — 8" h.p., BK, #0771-571, 1965–1972 (Wendy Ann).......................... 135.00
    BKW, #771 (Wendy Ann) 175.00
    8" h.p., straight legs, #571, 1973–1976, marked "Alex" 65.00
    8" h.p., straight legs, #571, 1976–1986 (1985–1986 white face) 50.00
ARIES — 8", #21330, 1998, gray furry ram outfit 90.00
ARMENIA — 8", #507, 1989–1990 (Wendy Ann) 70.00
ARRIVING IN AMERICA — 8" h.p., #326, 1992–1993 only, Americana Series (Wendy Ann).......... 85.00
ARTIE — 12" plastic/vinyl, 1962, sold through FAO Schwarz (Smarty) 285.00
ARTISTE WENDY —8", #31250, 1998–1999, pink smock and black beret 85.00
ASHLEY — 8", #628, 1990 only, Scarlett Series, tan jacket/hat............................ 95.00
    8" h.p., #633, 1991–1992 only, Scarlett Series, as Confederate officer 125.00
ASTOR — 9" early vinyl toddler, 1953 only, gold organdy dress & bonnet 150.00
ASTROLOGICAL MONTH DOLLS — 14–17" compo., 1938 (Wendy) 525.00
AUNT AGATHA — 8" h.p., #434, 1957 (Wendy Ann)...................................... 1,200.00 up
AUNT BETSY — Cloth/felt, 1930s 900.00
AUNT MARCH — 8", #14621, 1996 .... 70.00
AUNT PITTY PAT — 14–17" compo., 1939 (Wendy Ann) from "Gone with the Wind" .... 1,500.00 up
    8" h.p., #435, 1957 (Wendy Ann) from "Gone with the Wind"............................ 1,700.00 up
    8" h.p., straight leg, #636, 1991–1992, Scarlett Series 100.00
AUNTIE EM — 8" h.p., #14515, 1995 only, Wizard of Oz series 75.00
AUSTRALIA — 8", #504, 1990–1991 only (Wendy Ann) 55.00
AUSTRIA BOY * — 8" h.p., 1974–1989 (Wendy Ann)
    Straight legs, #599–#533, 1973–1975, marked "Alex" 70.00
    #599, 1976–1989, marked "Alexander" 50.00
AUSTRIA GIRL * — 8" h.p., 1974–1993 (Wendy Ann)
    Straight legs, #598, 1973–1975, marked "Alex"... 75.00
    #598–#532, 1976–1990, marked "Alexander" 50.00
    Reintroduced #110539 (Maggie), 1994 only... 65.00
AUTUMN — 14", 1993, Changing Seasons Doll with four outfits 150.00
AUTUMN IN N.Y. — (see First Modern Doll Club under Special Events/Exclusives)
AUTUMN LEAVES — 14", 1994, Classic Dolls.. 135.00
AVRIL, JANE — 10" (see Marshall Fields under Special Events/Exclusives)
* FORMERLY TYROLEAN BOY AND GIRL

A

················ PLEASE READ "WHAT IS A PRICE GUIDE?" FOR ADDITIONAL INFORMATION ·····················

BABBIE — Cloth with long thin legs, inspired by Katharine Hepburn............................ 1,000.00 up
    16", cloth child doll, 1934–1936 .... 775.00 up
    14" h.p. (Maggie)... 800.00 up
BABETTE — 10" Portrette, #1117, 1988–1989, black short dress (Cissette)................. 85.00
BABS — 20" h.p., 1949 (Maggie)....................................... 850.00
BABS SKATER — 18" compo. (Margaret)................................. 1,250.00 up
    15" h.p., 1948–1950 (Margaret)................................. 1,100.00 up
    17–18" h.p.. 1,250.00 up
    21" h.p.. 1,300.00 up
BABSIE BABY — Compo./cloth, moving tongue 550.00
BABSIE SKATER (ROLLER) — 15", 1941 (Princess Elizabeth)................. 750.00 up
BABY BETTY — 10–12" compo., 1935–1936................................. 300.00
BABY BROTHER AND SISTER — 20", cloth/vinyl, 1977–1979 (Mary Mine)................. 125.00 each
    14", 1979–1982 .... 85.00 each
    14", re-introduced 1989 only .... 65.00 each
BABY CLOWN — See Clowns
BABY ELLEN — 14", 1965–1972 (black Sweet Tears) 125.00
BABY GENIUS — 11" all cloth, 1930s 425.00
    11–12" compo./cloth, 1930s–1940s............................... 225.00 up
    16" compo./cloth, 1930s–1940s 250.00
    22", compo./cloth, 1940s 550.00
    15", 18", h.p. head, vinyl limbs, 1949–1950 (some get sticky or turn dark)............... 100.00–150.00
    21" h.p. head, vinyl limbs, 1952–1955 .... 375.00
    8" h.p./vinyl, 1956–1962 (see Little Genius)
BABY JANE — 16" compo., 1935 .... 950.00 up
BABY LYNN — 20" cloth/vinyl, 1973–1976................................. 135.00
    14" cloth/vinyl, 1973–1976 .... 125.00
BABY MADISON — 14", #29750, 1999, vinyl, with layette 105.00
BABY McGUFFEY — 22–24" compo., 1937 .... 300.00
    20" cloth/vinyl, 1971–1976 .... 175.00
    14" cloth/vinyl, 1972–1978 .... 150.00
BABY PRECIOUS — 14" cloth/vinyl, 1975 only 100.00
    21" cloth/vinyl, 1974–1976 .... 150.00
BABY IN LOUIS VUITTON TRUNK/WARDROBE OR WICKER BASKET WITH LEGS — Any year .... 900.00 up
BABY SHAVER — 12", cloth h.p., 1941–1943, yellow floss wig, round painted eyes (Little Shaver) ..... 650.00 up
BAD LITTLE GIRL — 16" cloth, 1966 only, blue dress, eyes and mouth turned down, looking sad........ 250.00
BALI — 8" h.p., #533, 1993 only 70.00
BALLERINA — (Also see individual dolls – Leslie, Margaret, etc.)
    9" compo., 1935–1941 (Little Betty) 350.00
    11–13", 1930s (Betty).. 375.00
    11–14" compo., 1936–1938 (Wendy Ann) 425.00
    17" compo., 1938–1941 (Wendy Ann) .... 600.00 up
    21" compo., 1947, "Debra" ("Deborah") Portrait ballerina in mint condition (Wendy Ann)...... 5,000.00 up
    8" h.p., must have excellent face color. (Wendy Ann)
    (Also see Enchanted Doll House under Special Events/Exclusives)
    (Also see M.A.D.C. under Special Events/Exclusives)
        SLNW, #354, 1953–1954, lavender, yellow, pink, or blue............. 700.00 up
          8" straight leg, #0730, #530, #430, 1973–1992 (1985–1987 white face)................ 85.00
        SLW, #454, 1955, lavender, yellow, pink, or white .... 650.00 up
        BKW, #564, 1954–1960, golden yellow 550.00

B

        #454, 1955, white 475.00
        #564, 1956, rose 600.00
        #564–631, 1956, yellow 650.00
        #364, 1957, blue 400.00
        #544, 1958, pink 375.00
        #420, 1959, gold 750.00
        #420, 1961, lavender 725.00
        #640, 1964, pink 450.00
    BK, #620-730, 1965–1972, yellow 375.00
        #440-730, 1962–1972, blue 250.00
        #440-730, 1962–1972, pink 225.00
    SLNW, #330, 1990–1991 (black or white dolls, 1991), Americana Series, white/gold outfit (Wendy Ann) . . . 75.00
        #331–331-1, 1992, black or white doll in pink/silver outfit (Wendy Ann) 65.00
        #331, 1993, white doll only pink/silver outfit 60.00
        #100331, 1994-1995, white doll, pink tutu 65.00
        #13900 – 1998, lace tutu over pink tulle 85.00
        #17640, 1999, blue Ballet Recital, wears silver crown 75.00
        #17650, 1999, lilac Ballet Recital, silver tutu 75.00
        #17690, 1999, pink Ballet Recital, pink knit outfit 70.00
    10–11" h.p., #813, 1957–1960, must have excellent face color (Cissette) 375.00
    12", 1964 only (Janie) 300.00
    12", 1989–1990, "Muffin," (Janie) 85.00
    12", 1990–1992 only, Romance Collection (Nancy Drew) 85.00
    12", 1993 only, in lavender (Lissy) 150.00
    14", 1963 only (Melinda) . . . . 325.00 up
    15–18" h.p., 1950–1952, must have good face color (Margaret) 625.00–725.00
    16½" h.p., 1957–1964 jointed ankles, knees & elbows, must have good face color (Elise) 375.00
        1957, yellow, rare 850.00
        1958, white 375.00
        1959, gold 395.00
        1960, pink 350.00
        1961, upswept hairdo, pink 400.00
        1962, blue 350.00
        1963–1964 only, small flowers in 1963; large flowers in 1964 (Marybel) (18" also Elise) 400.00

Cissette Ballerina, 10", #813, 1960, hard plastic. Original vinyl pointed ballet shoes.

Ruth, 8", Bible character, h.p. 1954 only, all original. Very rare doll.

17" plastic/vinyl, 1967–1989, discontinued costume (Elise)............................150.00
17" plastic/vinyl, 1990–1991, "Firebird" and "Swan Lake" (Elise)........................150.00
17", 1966–1971 only (Leslie - black doll) 400.00
BARBARA JANE — 29" cloth/vinyl, 1952 only, mint......................................500.00
BARBARA LEE — 8", 1955, name given by FAO Schwarz 650.00
BARBARY COAST — 10" h.p., 1962–1963, Portrette (Cissette) ....1,500.00 up
BARTON, CLARA — 10", #1130, 1989 only, Portrette, wears nurse's outfit (Cissette) 125.00
BASEBALL BOY — 8", #16313, 1997, red, white baseball outfit 60.00
BASEBALL GIRL — 8", #16300, baseball outfit with ball glove...........................60.00
BATHING BEAUTY — (see U.F.D.C. under Special Events/Exclusives)
BEAST — 12", 1992 only, Romance Series (Nancy Drew) 100.00
    8" #140487 Storyland Series - 1994, Fairy Tales Series - 1995 ....70.00
BEAU BRUMMEL — Cloth, 1930s 750.00
BEAUTY — 12", 1992 only, Romance Series (Nancy Drew) 100.00
    8" #140486 Storyland Series - 1994, Fairy Tales Series - 1995 ....80.00
BEAUTY QUEEN — 10" h.p., 1961 only (Cissette) 325.00
BEAUX ARTS DOLLS — 18" h.p., 1953 only (Margaret, Maggie)......................2,000.00 up
BEDDY-BYE BROOKE — (see FAO Schwarz under Special Events/Exclusives)
BEDDY-BYE BRENDA (Brooke's sister) (see FAO Schwarz under Special Events/Exclusives)
BEING A PROM QUEEN — (see Wendy Loves)
BEING JUST LIKE MOMMY — (See Wendy Loves)
BELGIUM — 8" h.p., BK, #762, 1972 only (Wendy Ann) 125.00
    8" straight legs, #0762, #562, 1973–1975, marked "Alex" 70.00
    8" straight legs, #562, 1976–1988, marked "Alexander" 60.00
    7" compo., 1935–1938 (Tiny Betty) 275.00
    9" compo., 1936 only (Little Betty) 300.00
BELLE — 14", #18402, 1996 Dickens, red jacket, long skirt 125.00
BELLE BRUMMEL — Cloth, 1930s...775.00
BELLE OF THE BALL — 10", #1120, 1989 only, Portrette, deep rose gown (Cissette) 130.00
BELLE WATLING — 10", 1992 only, Scarlett Series (Cissette).............................125.00
    21", #16277, 1995 only, red outfit
        with fur trim (Jacqueline) 325.00
BELLOWS' ANNE — 14" plastic/vinyl, #1568, 1987 only,
    Fine Arts Series 85.00
BELK & LEGGETT DEPARTMENT STORES — (see Special Events/Exclusives)
BERNHARDT, SARAH — 21", #2249, 1987 only,
    dressed in all burgundy 325.00
BESSY BELL — 14" plastic/vinyl, #1565, 1988 only,
    Classic Series (Mary Ann) 75.00
BESSY BROOKS — 8", #487, 1988–1991,
    Storybook Series (Wendy Ann) 65.00
    8", 1990 (see Collectors United/Bride under
        Special Events/Exclusives)
BEST MAN — 8" h.p., #461, 1955 only (Wendy Ann) 825.00
BETH — (see Little Women)
    10" (see Spiegel's under Special Events/Exclusives)
BETTY — 14" compo., 1935–1942 ....425.00
    12" compo., 1936–1937 only 350.00
    16–18" compo., 1935–1942 ....425.00
    19–21" compo., 1938–1941 ....500.00
    14½–17½" h.p., 1951 only, made for Sears (Maggie) 550.00
    30" plastic/vinyl, 1960 only 400.00
BETTY, TINY — 7" compo., 1934–1943 ....300.00 up
BETTY, LITTLE — 9" compo., 1935–1943 ....325.00 up
BETTY BLUE — 8" straight leg, #420, 1987–1988 only,
    Storybook Series (Maggie) 75.00
BETTY BOOP — 10", #17500, (Cissette) red dress, 1999 .....130.00

Sarah Bernhardt, 21", #2249, 1987, (Jacqueline). Lovely burgundy gown and hat.

BIBLE CHARACTER DOLLS — 8" h.p., 1954 only, (Wendy Ann)
(Mary of Bethany, David, Martha, Ruth, Timothy, Rhoda, Queen Esther and Joseph) . . . . 7,000.00 up
1995 (see Delilah, Joseph, Queen Esther, and Samson)
BILL/BILLY — 8" h.p., #320, #567, #420, 1955–1963, has boy's clothes and hair style (Wendy Ann) . . . . 475.00 up
#577, 464, #466, #421, #442, #488, #388, 1953–1957, as groom . . . . 500.00 up
BILLIE HOLIDAY — 10", #22070, 1997, silver long gown 110.00
BILLY-IN-THE-BOX — 8" jester, 1996, Alexander signature box 125.00
BINNIE — 18" plastic/vinyl toddler, 1964 only 375.00
BINNIE WALKER — 15–18" h.p., 1954–1955 only (Cissy) 175.00–350.00
15", 1955 only, in trunk with wardrobe 750.00
15", 1955 only, h.p. skater . . . . 650.00 up
18", toddler, plastic/vinyl, 1964 only . . . . 325.00 up
25", 1955 only in formals, ... 500.00 up
25", h.p., 1954–1955 only, dresses 450.00
BIRDS, THE – 10", #14800, green dress, fur coat pictured 1998 catalog . . . . Not available for sale
BIRTHDAY DOLLS — 7" compo., 1937–1939 (Tiny Betty) . . . . 350.00 up
BIRTHDAY, HAPPY — 1985 (see M.A.D.C. under Special Events/Exclusives)
BITSEY — 11–12" compo., 1942–1946 . . . . 250.00
11–16" with h.p. head, 1949–1951 . . . . 250.00
19–26", 1949–1951 . . . . 165.00–275.00
12" cloth/vinyl, 1965–1966 only 150.00
BITSEY, LITTLE — 9" all vinyl, 1967–1968 only 125.00
11–16" 75.00–175.00
BLACK FOREST — 8", #512, 1989–1990 (Wendy Ann) 75.00
BLISS, BETTY TAYLOR — 1979–1981, 2nd set Presidents' Ladies/ First Ladies Series (Mary Ann) 125.00
BLUE BOY — 16" cloth, 1930s 650.00
7" compo., 1936–1938 (Tiny Betty) 325.00
9" compo., 1938–1941 (Little Betty) 375.00
12" plastic/vinyl, #1340, 1972–1983, Portrait Children (Nancy Drew) 75.00
1985–1987, dressed in blue velvet 75.00
8", #22130, 1997 – 1998, blue satin outfit 70.00
BLUE DANUBE — 18" h.p., 1953 only, pink floral gown (#2001B - blue floral gown) (Maggie) . . . . 1,650.00 up
18" h.p., 1954 only, Me and My Shadow Series, blue taffeta dress (Margaret) . . . . 1,500.00 up
BLUE FAIRIE — 10", #1166, 1993 #201166, 1994, Portrette, character from Pinocchio (Cissette) 125.00
BLUE MOON — 14", #1560, 1991–1992 only, Classic Series (Louisa) 125.00
BLUE ZIRCON — 10", #1153, 1992 only, Birthday Collection, gold/blue flapper 100.00
BLYNKIN — (see Dutch Lullaby)
BOBBY — 8" h.p., #347, 1957 only (Wendy Ann) 575.00
8" h.p., #361, #320, 1960 only (Maggie Mixup) 600.00
BOBBY Q. — Cloth, 1940–1942 . . . . 750.00
BOBBY (BOBBIE) SOXER — 8" h.p., 1990–1991 (see Disney under Special Events/Exclusives)
BOBO CLOWN — 8", #320, 1991–1992, Americana Series (Wendy Ann) 75.00
BOHEMIA — 8", #508, 1989–1991 (Wendy Ann) 60.00
BOLIVIA 8" h.p., BK & BKW, #786, 1963–1966 (Wendy Ann) 350.00
BONNET TOP WENDY — 8", #14487, 1995, Toy Shelf Series, yarn braids and large bonnet 65.00
BONNIE (BABY) — 16–19" vinyl, 1954–1955 . . . . 125.00
24–30", 1954–1955 . . . . 125.00–250.00
BONNIE BLUE — 14", #1305, 1989 only, Jubilee II (Mary Ann) 125.00
8" h.p., #629, #630, 1990–1992 (Wendy Ann) 110.00
8", #16649, 1995, side saddle riding outfit 85.00
BONNIE GOES TO LONDON — 8", #640, 1993, Scarlett Series #160640-1994 . . . . 95.00
BONNIE TODDLER — 18" cloth/h.p. head/vinyl limbs, 1950–1951 . . . . 175.00
19" all vinyl, 1954–1955 . . . . 200.00
23–24" 250.00
BON VOYAGE — 8" and 10" (see I. Magnum under Special Events/Exclusives)
BOONE, DANIEL — 8" h.p., #315, 1991 only, Americana Series, has no knife (Wendy Ann) 70.00

B

Bo Peep, Little — 7" compo., 1937–1941, Storybook Series (Tiny Betty) 375.00
    9–11" compo., 1936–1940 (Little Betty, Wendy Ann) 350.00
    7½" h.p., SLW, #489, 1955 only (Wendy Ann) 575.00
    8" h.p., BKW, #383, 1962–1964 (Wendy Ann) 295.00
    8" h.p., BK, #783, 1965–1972 (Wendy Ann) 125.00
    8" h.p., straight leg, #0783-483, 1973–1975, marked "Alex" (Wendy Ann) 75.00
    8" h.p., 1976–1986, #483–#486, marked "Alexander" (Wendy Ann) 65.00
    14", #1563, 1988–1989, Classic Series (Mary Ann) 75.00
    14", #1567, 1992–1993 only, candy stripe pink dress (Mary Ann) 125.00
    12" porcelain, #009, 1990–1992 . . . . 225.00
    10" Portrette series, 1994 . . . . 100.00
    8" (see Dolly Dears under Special Events/Exclusives)
Boys Choir of Harlem — 8", #20170, 1997 – 1998, maroon blazer, Kufi hat 75.00
Brazil — 7" compo., 1937–1943 (Tiny Betty) 300.00
    9" compo., 1938–1940 (Little Betty) 300.00
    8" h.p., BKW, #773, 1965–1972 (Wendy Ann) 125.00
      BK, #773 . . . . 100.00
    8" h.p., straight leg, #0773, #573, 1973–1975, marked "Alex" (Wendy Ann) 70.00
    8" h.p., straight leg, #573, #547, #530, 1976–1988, marked "Alexander". 60.00
      #573, #547, #530, 1985–1987 . . . . 60.00
    8" straight leg, #11564, 1996 international, carnival costume. 65.00
Brenda Starr — 12" h.p., 1964 only (became "Yolanda" in 1965) 250.00
    Bride. 300.00
    Street dresses 225.00
    Ball gown 375.00
    Beach outfit 225.00
    Raincoat/hat/dress. 250.00
Briar Rose — (see M.A.D.C. under Special Events/Exclusives)
    10", #14101, 1995, Brothers Grimm Series, blue floral with apron (Cissette) 95.00
Brick Piggy — 12", #10010, 1997, denim overalls, maize felt cap 85.00
Bride —

Bo Peep, 14", #1563, 1988 – 1989 (Mary Ann). Classic Series.

    Tiny Betty: Composition 7" compo., 1935–1939 . . . . . .275.00
        9–11" compo., 1936–1941 (Little Betty) 300.00
    Wendy Ann: Composition 13", 14", 15" compo., 1935–1941
        (Wendy Ann) 275.00–375.00
        17–18" compo., 1935–1943 (Wendy Ann) 450.00
        21–22" compo., 1942–1943 (Wendy Ann) . . . . .600.00 up
        In trunk/trousseau (Wendy Ann) . . . . .1,650.00 up
        21" compo., 1945–1947, Royal Wedding/Portrait
        (Wendy Ann) . . . . .2,400.00 up
    Margaret, Maggie: Hard plastic
        15" h.p., 1951–1955 (Margaret) 675.00
        17" h.p., 1950, in pink (Margaret) 850.00
        18" h.p., tagged "Prin. Elizabeth" (Margaret) 675.00
        18" h.p., 1949–1955 (Maggie, Margaret) 675.00
        21" h.p., 1949–1953 (Margaret, Maggie) . . . . .1,200.00 up
        18"–21", pink bride, 1953 (Margaret) . . . . .950.00 up
        23" h.p. 1949, 1952–1955 (Margaret) 750.00
        25" h.p., 1955 only (Margaret) 825.00
    Elise: 16½" h.p., 1957–1964, jointed ankle, elbows & knees,
      must have good face color (also see 17" below)
        1957, nylon tulle, chapel length veil 375.00
        1958, wreath pattern hem of skirt 450.00
        1959, tulle puffed sleeves, long veil (pink) 625.00
        1960, satin gown, lace bodice with sequins & breads . .400.00
        1961, short bouffant hair, tulle with puff sleeves 375.00

B

B

1962, lace pattern bodice & trim on tulle skirt 400.00
1963, tulle, rows of lace on bodice. 425.00
1964, lace bodice & sleeves, lace on skirt, chapel length veil. 400.00

Cissy: 20" h.p., 1955–1958
1955 only, Dreams Come True Series, brocade gown with floor length veil . . . . 1,000.00 up
1956 only, tulle gown, tulle cap & chapel length veil, Fashion Parade Series . . . . 700.00 up
1957 only, Models Formal Gowns series,nylon tulle with double train of satin . . . . 675.00 up
1958 only, Dolls To Remember series, lace circles near hem (wreath pattern). . . . . 725.00 up
1959 only, tulle over white satin 450.00

Cissette: 10" h.p., 1957–1963 must have good face color
1957, tulle gown, short veil or lace & tulle cap veil 350.00
1958, lace wreath pattern, matches Elise & Cissy 425.00
1959–1960, tulle gown, puff sleeves 350.00
1961, tulle, rhinestones on collar & veil 375.00
1962, lace bodice & trim on skirt, long veil 350.00
1963, tulle, rows of lace on bodice & at hem (matches Elise the same year) 375.00
In trunk/trousseau, various years . . . . 900.00 up
#1136, 1990–1991, Portrette 125.00
#14103, 1995, 1920s style 100.00
#22470, 10" Empire Bride, 1998, lace gown, straw bonnet. 140.00
#22460, 10" Rococo Bride, 1998, peach gown, lace train 145.00
#22480, 10" Victorian Bride, 1998, blue satin gown 140.00

Lissy: 12" h.p., 1956–1959
1956, jointed knees & elbows, tulle, tulle cap veil 475.00
1957, same as 1956, except long veil 425.00
1958–1959, dotted net, tulle veil 475.00
Porcelain, 1991–1992 only (version of 14" head) 225.00

Jacqueline: 21" Portrait
#2151, 1965, full lace, wide lace edge on veil (Jacqueline) 900.00
#2192, 1969, full lace overskirt and plain veil 725.00

Alexander-kin (Wendy Ann): 8" h.p. or plastic/vinyl
8" h.p., #315, 1953 only, Quiz-kin . . . . 650.00 up
8" h.p., 1954 . . . . .600.00 up

Bride, 21", #2192, 1969 (Jacqueline). One of the 1969 Portrait dolls on cover of catalog.

Bunny, 18", 1962 only, plastic/vinyl. Original clothes.

SLW, BKW, #735 in 1955, #615 in 1956, #410 in 1957; #582 in 1958 . .375.00–475.00
BKW, #482, 1959, pink . . . . .1,000.00 up
BKW, #735, 1960 . . . . .375.00
BKW, #480, 1961 . . . . .350.00
BKW, #760 (#630 in 1965),
    1963–1965 . . . . .325.00
BK, #470 in 1966; #735
    in 1967–1972 . . . . .175.00
Straight leg, #0735-435, 1973–1975,
    marked "Alex" 100.00
Straight leg, #435, 1976–1994,
    marked "Alexander" 75.00
#337, white doll; #336-1, black doll,
    1991–1992 . . . . .65.00
#337, 1993, white only 60.00
#435, 1985–1987 . . . . .55.00
Collectors United (see under Special
Events/Exclusives) First Comes Love
#10395, 1995,
    Special Occasion Series 65.00
#10392, 1995, Special Occasion Series,
    three hair colors 65.00

#17016, 1996 white lace and satin gown 65.00
#21030, 1997 – 1998, white gown, comes with cake top, 21033 – African American 100.00
#21171, 1999, blonde or brunette, satin ribbon at hem 80.00
MARY ANN, JENNIFER, LOUISA: 14" plastic/vinyl
#1465 (#1565 in 1974, #1565 in 1977, #1570 in 1976), 1973–1977 (Mary Ann) 100.00
#1589 in 1987–1988; #1534 in 1990, Classic Series (Mary Ann, Jennifer) 100.00
#1566, reintroduced 1992 only, ecru gown (Louisa, Jennifer) 150.00
ELISE, LESLIE, POLLY: 17" plastic/vinyl or 21" porcelain
1966–1988 (Elise) 165.00
1966–1971 (Leslie) 325.00
1965–1970 (Polly) 275.00
Porcelain, 1989–1990, satin and lace look like bustle 425.00
Porcelain, Portrait Series, 1993–1994 . . . . 425.00
BRIDESMAID — 9" compo., 1937–1939 (Little Betty) 325.00
11–14" compo., 1938–1942 (Wendy Ann) 325.00–450.00
15–18" compo., 1939–1944 (Wendy Ann) 375.00–600.00
20–22" compo., 1941–1947, Portrait (Wendy Ann) . . . . 1,800.00 up
21½" compo., 1938–1941 (Princess Elizabeth) . . . . 950.00 up
15–17" h.p., 1950–1952 (Margaret, Maggie) 450.00–700.00
15" h.p., 1952 (Maggie) 550.00
18" h.p., 1952 (Maggie) 650.00
21" h.p., 1950–1953, side part mohair wig, deep pink or lavender gown (Margaret) . . . . 750.00 up
19" rigid vinyl, in pink, 1952–1953 (Margaret) . . . . 550.00 up
15" h.p., 1955 only (Cissy, Binnie) 325.00
18" h.p., 1955 only (Cissy, Binnie) 350.00
25" h.p., 1955 only (Cissy, Binnie) 475.00
20" h.p., 1956 only, Fashion Parade Series, blue nylon tulle & net (Cissy) . . . . 1,000.00 up
10" h.p., 1957–1963 (Cissette) 375.00
12" h.p., 1956–1959 (Lissy) . . . . 650.00 up
16½" h.p., 1957–1959 (Elise) . . . . 450.00 up
8", h.p. SLNW, 1953, pink, blue, or yellow . . . . 900.00 up
8" h.p., SLW, #478, 1955 (Wendy Ann) . . . . 700.00 up
BKW, #621, 1956 . . . . 675.00 up
BKW, #408, #583, #445, 1957–1959 . . . . 700.00 up
17" plastic/vinyl (Elise) 1966–1987 . . . . 175.00

Elise Bridesmaid, 16½", #1830, 1959. Pleated nylon and flowers on bodice and waist. Picture hat with flowers. Hard plastic with vinyl arms and jointed elbows, knees, and ankles.

Lissy Bridesmaid, 12", 1957, #1161. All hard plastic. Shown is the rare lavender Bridesmaid dress and hat.

17" plastic/vinyl, 1966–1971 (Leslie) 325.00
BRIGITTA — 11" & 14" (see Sound of Music)
BROOKE — (see FAO Schwarz under Special Events/Exclusives)
BUBBLES CLOWN — 8" h.p., #342, 1993–1994, Americana Series 75.00
BUCK RABBIT — Cloth/felt, 1930s . . . . 650.00 up
BUD — 16–19" cloth/vinyl, 1952 only (Rosebud head) 175.00
19" & 25", 1952–1953 only 175.00–275.00
BULGARIA — 8", #557, 1986–1987, white face (Wendy Ann) 60.00
BUMBLE BEE — 8" h.p., #323, 1992–1993, only Americana Series 75.00
BUNNY — 18" plastic/vinyl, 1962 only, mint 250.00
BURMA — 7" compo., 1939–1943 (Tiny Betty) 350.00
BUTCH — 11–12" compo./cloth, 1942–1946 . . . . 150.00
14–16" compo./cloth, 1949–1951 . . . . 175.00
14" cloth, vinyl head & limbs, 1950 only 175.00
12" cloth/vinyl, 1965–1966 only 125.00
BUTCH, LITTLE — 9" all vinyl, 1967–1968 only 125.00
BUTCH McGUFFEY — 22" compo./cloth, 1940–1941 . . . . 275.00

C

PLEASE READ "WHAT IS A PRICE GUIDE?" FOR ADDITIONAL INFORMATION

C.U. — (see Collectors United under Special Events/Exclusives)
CAFE ROSE AND IVORY COCKTAIL DRESS — 10", #22200 – white, #22203 – black, 1997 – 1998. . . . . 125.00
CALAMITY JANE — 8" h.p. Americana Series, 1994 only (Wendy Ann) 75.00
CALLA LILLY — 10", #22390, 1998 (Cissette), white gown, hand beaded jewels 230.00
CAMEO LADY — (see Collectors United under Special Events/Exclusives)
CAMELOT — (see Collectors United under Special Events/Exclusives)
CAMILLE — 21" compo., 1938–1939 (Wendy Ann) . . . . 3,500.00 up
CANADA — 8" h.p., BK, #760, 1968–1972 (Wendy Ann). 100.00
Straight leg, #0706, 1973–1975, marked "Alex" 65.00
Straight legs, #560 (#534 in 1986), 1976–1988 (white face 1985–1987), marked "Alexander". 60.00
Straight legs, #24130, 1999, hockey skater. 90.00
CANCER — 8", #21360, 1998, red crab costume. 90.00
CANDY KID — 11–15" compo., 1938–1941 (Wendy Ann) red/white stripe dress 275.00–450.00
CAPRICORN — 8", #21300, 1998 (Maggie) fuchsia snakeskin body 90.00
CAPTAIN HOOK — 8" h.p., #478, 1992–1993 only, Storyland Series (Peter Pan) (Wendy Ann) 100.00
CAREEN — (see Carreen)
CARMEN — Dressed like Carmen Miranda, but not marked or meant as such.
7" compo., 1938–1943 (Tiny Betty) 350.00
9–11" compo., 1938–1943, boy & girl (see also "Rumbera/Rumbero") (Little Betty). . . . . 275.00 each
11" compo., 1937–1939, has sleep eyes (Little Betty) 350.00
14" compo., 1937–1940 (Wendy Ann) 450.00
17" compo., 1939–1942 (Wendy Ann) 650.00
21" compo., 1939–1942, extra makeup, mint (Wendy Ann) . . . . 1,400.00 up
21" compo., 1939–1942, Portrait with extra make-up . . . . 1,050.00 up
14" plastic/vinyl, #1410, 1983–1986, Opera Series (Mary Ann) 80.00
10" h.p., #1154, 1993 only, Portrette Series (Miranda), yellow/red. 90.00
CARNAVALE DOLL — (see FAO Schwarz under Special Events/Exclusives)
CARNIVAL IN RIO — 21" porcelain, 1989–1990 . . . . 500.00
CARNIVAL IN VENICE — 21" porcelain, 1990–1991 . . . . 500.00
CAROLINE — 15" vinyl, 1961–1962 only, in dresses, pants/jacket 375.00
In riding habit 375.00
Dressed as Kurt of Sound of Music. 475.00

In case/wardrobe . . . . 900.00 up
   8", 1993 (see Belk & Leggett under Special Events/Exclusives)
   8", 1994 (see Neiman-Marcus under Special Events/Exclusives)
CARREEN/CAREEN — 14–17" compo., #1593, 1937–1938 (Wendy Ann) . . . . 700.00 up
   14" plastic/vinyl, 1992–1993 only (Louisa/Jennifer). 125.00
   8" plaid, two large ruffles at hem, #160646, 1994 only. 95.00
   8", #15190, 1999 (Wendy) lavender dress, straw hat 80.00
CARROT KATE — 14", #25506, 1995, Ribbons & Bows Series, vegetable print dress (Mary Ann) 150.00
CARROT TOP — 21" cloth, 1967 only 125.00
CASEY JONES — 8" h.p., 1991–1992 only, Americana Series 70.00
CASPER'S FRIEND WENDY — 8", (Maggie) #15210, 1999, red costume, broom 80.00
CATERPILLAR — 8" h.p., #14594, 1995 – 1996, has eight legs, Alice In Wonderland Series 85.00
CATS — 16", plush, dressed, glass eyes, long lashes, felt nose 350.00
CAT ON A HOT TIN ROOF — 10", #20011, "Maggie," white chiffon dress. 115.00
CELIA'S DOLLS — (see Special Events/Exclusives)
CENTURY OF FASHION — 14" & 18" h.p., 1954 (Margaret, Maggie & Cissy) . . . . 1,800.00 up
CHANGING SEASONS — (Spring, Summer, Autumn, Winter) 14" 1993–1994 . . . . 150.00 each
CHARITY — 8" h.p., #485, 1961 only, Americana Series, blue cotton dress (Wendy Ann) . . . . 1,900.00 up
CHAMPS-ELYSÉES — 21" h.p., black lace over pink, rhinestone on cheek . . . . 4,800.00 up
CHARLENE — 18" cloth/vinyl, 1991–1992 only 100.00
CHATTERBOX — 24" plastic/vinyl talker, 1961 only . . . . 275.00 up
CHEERLEADER — 8", #324, 1990–1991 only, Americana Series (Wendy Ann) 65.00
   8", 1990 (see I. Magnin under Special Events/Exclusives)
   8" h.p., #324, #324-1, 1992–1993 only, Americana Series, black or white doll, royal blue/gold outfit . . . 70.00
CHEF ALEX — 8", #31260, 1998 (Maggie) chef attire. 85.00
CHERI — 18" h.p., 1954 only, Me and My Shadow Series,
   white satin gown, pink opera coat (Margaret). . . . . 1,600.00 up
CHERRY BLOSSOM — 14", #25504, 1995, Ribbons & Bows Series, cherry print dress (Mary Ann) 135.00
CHERRY GIRL — 8", #17590, 1999, Mary Engelbreit, comes with basket and card. 70.00
CHERRY TWINS — 8" h.p., #300E, 1957 only (Wendy Ann) . . . . 1,600.00 up each
   8", BK, #17700, 1999, pair, remake of 1957 set 130.00
CHERUB — 12" vinyl, 1960–1961. . . . . 250.00
   18" h.p. head/cloth & vinyl, 1950s. 350.00
   26", 1950s 375.00
CHERUB BABIES — Cloth, 1930s 450.00
CHESHIRE CAT — 8", #13070, 1997 – 1999 storyland series, pink velvet cat suit 60.00
CHILE — 8" h.p., #528, 1992 only (Maggie) 65.00
CHILD AT HEART SHOP — (see Special Events/Exclusives)
CHILD'S ANGEL — 8", #14701, 1996, gold wings, harp, halo 65.00
CHINA — 7" compo., 1936–1940 (Tiny Betty) 300.00
   9" compo., 1935–1938 (Little Betty) 275.00
   8" h.p., BK, #772, 1972 (Wendy Ann) 100.00
   8" (Maggie smile face) 125.00
   Straight leg, #0772–#572, 1973–1975, marked "Alex" 70.00
   Straight leg, #572, 1976–1986, marked "Alexander" (Wendy Ann). 60.00
      #572, 1987–1989 (Maggie). 65.00
   8", #11550, 1995 only, 3 painted lashes at edge of eyes (Wendy Ann). 60.00
   8", #11561, 1996 International, Little Empress costume. 75.00
CHINESE NEW YEAR — 8", 2 dolls, #21040, 1997 – 1998 . . . . 130.00
   8", 3 dolls, dragon, #21050, 1997 – 1998 . . . . 230.00
CHRISTENING BABY — 11–13" cloth/vinyl, 1951–1954 . . . . 135.00
   16–19" 150.00
CHRISTMAS ANGELS — (see Tree Toppers)
CHRISTMAS CANDY — 14" #1544, 1993 only, Classic Series 115.00
CHRISTMAS CAROL — 8" (see Saks Fifth Avenue under Special Events/Exclusives)
CHRISTMAS CAROLER — 8" #19650, 1997, red velvet cape, print skirt 85.00
CHRISTMAS CAROLING — 10", #1149, 1992–1993 only, Portrette, burnt orange/gold dress. 115.00

CHRISTMAS COOKIE — 14", #1565, 1992 (Also see Lil Christmas Cookie, 8") (Louisa/Jennifer). 125.00
CHRISTMAS EVE — 14" plastic/vinyl #241594, 1994 only (Mary Ann) 115.00
    8", #10364, 1995, Christmas Series. 75.00
CHRISTMAS HOLLY – 8", #19680, 1998–1999, print dress, red coat 85.00
CHRISTMAS SHOPPE — (see Special Events/Exclusives)
CHRISTMAS TREE TOPPER — 8" (see Spiegel's under Special Events/Exclusives; also Tree Topper)
CHURCHILL, LADY — 18" h.p., #2020C, 1953 only, Beaux Arts Series,
    pink gown with full opera coat (Margaret). . . . . 2,200.00 up
CHURCHILL, SIR WINSTON — 18" h.p., 1953 only, has hat (Margaret) . . . . 1,200.00 up
CINDERELLA — (see also Topsy Turvy for two headed version)
    7–8" compo., 1935–1944 (Tiny Betty). 300.00
    9" compo., 1936–1941 (Little Betty) 350.00
    13" compo., 1935–1937 (Wendy Ann) 375.00
    14" compo., 1939 only, Sears exclusive (Princess Elizabeth) 500.00
    15" compo., 1935–1937 (Betty) 475.00
    16–18" compo., 1935–1939 (Princess Elizabeth) . . . . 500.00 up
    8" h.p., #402, 1955 only (Wendy Ann) 950.00
    8" h.p., #498, 1990–1991, Storyland Series (Wendy Ann). 65.00
    8", #476, 1992–1993, blue ballgown, #140476, 1994 Storyland Series. 75.00
    8", #475, 1992 only, "Poor" outfit in blue w/black strips 70.00
    8" h.p., #14540, 1995–1996, pink net gown with roses, Brothers Grimm Series, #13400, 1997–1999 . . . . . 75.00
    8", h.p., #13410, 1997–1999, calico skirt with broom and pumpkin. 75.00
    8", h.p., #13490, 1999, Cinderella's wedding, white gown 90.00
    12" h.p., 1966 only, Literature Series (classic Lissy). . . . . 950.00 up
    12" h.p., 1966, "Poor" outfit 650.00
        1966, in window box with both outfits. 1,500.00
    14" h.p., 1950–1951, ballgown (Margaret). . . . . 850.00 up

Cissette, 10", #815, 1958, hard plastic.

Cissette, 10", 1961, original tagged outfit.

Cissette, #838, 1958, hard plastic. A vision in pink with rhinestones and perfect little flowers.

Cinderella, 14", #1546, plastic/vinyl (Mary Ann). Made from 1988 – 1989.

Cissette, #974, 10", 1957, hard plastic.

Cissette, 10", #815, 1958, hard plastic.

CINDERELLA, CONTINUED...

14" h.p., 1950–1951, "Poor" outfit (Margaret)	600.00
18" h.p., 1950–1951 (Margaret)	750.00
21", #45501, 1995, pink and blue, Madame's Portfolio Series	300.00
14" plastic/vinyl (#1440 to 1974; #1504 to 1991; #1541 in 1992) 1967–1992, "Poor" outfit (can be green, blue, gray or brown) (Mary Ann)	80.00
14", #140 on box, 1969 only, FAO Schwarz, all blue satin/gold trim, mint (Mary Ann)	425.00
14" plastic/vinyl, #1445, #1446, #1546, #1548, 1970–1983, Classic Series, dressed in pink (Mary Ann)	125.00
#1548, #1549, 1984–1986, blue ballgown, two styles (Mary Ann)	125.00
14", #1546, #1547, 1987–1991, Classic Series, white or blue ballgown (Mary Ann, Jennifer)	150.00
14", #1549, 1992 only, white/gold ballgown (Jennifer)	150.00
14", 1985, with trunk (see Enchanted Dollhouse under Special Events/Exclusives)	
14", 1994, has two outfits (see Disney World under Special Events/Exclusives)	
14", 1996, #87002, white gown, gold crown (Mary Ann)	125.00
10", 1989 (see Disney Annual Showcase of Dolls under Special Events/Exclusives)	
10", #1137, 1990–1991, Portrette, dressed in all pink (Cissette)	100.00

CINDERELLA'S CARRIAGE — #13460, 1999, white metal carriage 175.00
CINDERELLA'S FOOTMOUSE — 8", #13470, 1999, painted face 105.00
CISSETTE — 10–11" h.p., 1957–1963, high heel feet, jointed elbows & knees, must have good face color,
  in various street dresses. Allow more for M.I.B., rare outfits & fancy hairdos. 275.00
  In formals, ballgowns . . . . 475.00 up
  Coats & hats 325.00
  1961 only, beauty queen with trophy 350.00
  Special gift set/three wigs 900.00
    Doll only, clean with good face color. 125.00
  1957, Queen/trunk/trousseau . . . . 1,200.00 up
    Slacks or pants outfits. 275.00
CISSETTE BARCELONA — 10", Spanish costume, black lace, 1999 . . . . 165.00
CISSY — 20" h.p. (also 21"), 1955–1959, jointed elbows & knees, high heel feet, must have good
  face color, in various street dresses. 375.00

C

Dating Cissette Dolls

Eyelids: 1975 - beige; 1958 - pale pink; 1959–1963 - peach

Clothes: 1957–1958 - darts in bodice; 1959–1963 - no darts except ballgowns

Fingernails: 1962–1963 - polished

Eyebrows: 1957–1963 - single stroked

Body and legs: 1957–1963 - head strung with hook and rubber band; legs jointed with plastic socket

Feet: 1957–1963 - high heels

Wigs: 1957–1958 - three rows of stitching; 1959–1963 - zigzag stitches except 1961–1962 with fancy hairdos, then three rows; 1963 - few have rooted hair in cap, glued to head or removable wigs

Tags: 1957–1962 - turquoise; 1963 - dark blue

PORTRETTE: 1968–1973
Two or three stroke eyebrows, blue eyelids, no earrings, strung head with hook, high heels.

JACQUELINE: 1961–1962
Two or three stroke eyebrows, side seam brunette wig, small curl on forehead, blue eyelids, eyeliner, painted lashes to sides of eyes, polished nails, head strung, socket jointed hips with side seams, high heels.

SLEEPING BEAUTY: 1959 ONLY
Three stroke eyebrows, pink eyelids, no earrings, mouth painted wider, no knee joints, flat feet, jointed with metal hooks.

SOUND OF MUSIC: 1971–1973
(Brigitta, Liesl, Louisa)
Two stroke eyebrows, the rest same as Portrettes.

TINKER BELL: 1969 ONLY
Two stroke eyebrows, blue eyelids, painted lashes to side of eyes, no earrings, hair rooted into wig cap, head and legs strung with metal hooks.

MARGOT: 1961
Same as Jacqueline, except has three stroke eyebrows and elaborate hairdos.

CISSY, CONTINUED...

Dress & full length coat	475.00
In ballgowns	850.00 up
Trunk/wardrobe	1,400.00 up
Pants suits	325.00
1950s magazine ads using doll (add 10.00 if framed)	25.00

21", reintroduced in the following 1996 MA Couture Collection

#67303, aquamarine evening column and coat	275.00
#67302, cafe rose and ivory cocktail dress	325.00
#67306, cafe rose and ivory cocktail dress, African-American	325.00
#67301, coral and leopard travel ensemble	325.00
#67601, ebony and ivory houndstooth suit	600.00
#67603, ebony and ivory houndstooth suit, African-American	600.00
#67304, onyx velvet lace gala gown and coat	350.00
#67602, pearl embroidered lace bridal gown	625.00
#86003, limited edition red sequined gown	375.00

21", 1997 MA Couture Collection

#22210, daisy resort ensemble	375.00
#22230, tea rose cocktail ensemble	350.00
#22220, calla lily evening ensemble	700.00

    #22240, peony and butterfly wedding gown 425.00
    #22290, gardenia gala ball gown 400.00
    #22250, Cissy's secret armoire trunk set (1997 – 1998) 735.00
  21", 1998 MA Couture (each limited to 1500)
    #22300 Cissy Paris, gold houndstooth outfit, sable, feathered hat 625.00
    #22330 Cissy Barcelona, coral charmeuse with black lace 625.00
    #22333 Cissy Barcelona, African-American 625.00
    #22320 Cissy Milan, long fur coat and fur-trimmed hat 625.00
    #22310 Cissy Venice, Brocade gown, blue taffeta cape 625.00
    #22340 Cissy Budapest, blue dress and coat trimmed with fur 625.00
  21", 1999, Cissy Designer Originals...(see Madame Alexander Doll Company under Specials/Exclusives)
CISSY BRIDE — 21", #52011, porcelain portrait, 1994 only 500.00
CISSY BY SCASSI — (see FAO Schwarz under Special Events/Exclusives)
CISSY GODEY BRIDE 21", #011, porcelain, 1993 only 525.00
CIVIL WAR — 18" h.p., #2010B, 1953 only, Glamour Girls Series, white taffeta with red roses (Margaret) . . . . 1,600.00 up
CLARA & THE NUTCRACKER — 14", #1564, 1992 only (Louisa/Jennifer) 110.00
CLARA'S PARTY DRESS — 8", #14570, 1995, Nutcracker Series 70.00
CLARABELL CLOWN — 19", 1951–1953 . . . . 350.00
    29" 575.00
    49" 1,000.00
CLASSIC BALLERINA — 16", #22700, white tulle and satin (1999) 170.00
CLASSIC BRIDE — 16", #22690, white tulle and lace gown (1999) 190.00
CLAUDETTE — 10", #1123 (in peach), 1988–1989, Portrette (Cissette) 100.00
CLEOPATRA — 12", #1315, 1980–1985, Portraits of History Series 75.00
    10", #86002, 1996 Platinum Collection 105.00
CLEVELAND, FRANCES — 1985–1987, 4th set Presidents' Ladies/First Ladies Series (Mary Ann) 125.00
CLOVER KID — 7" compo., 1935–1936 (Tiny Betty) 375.00
CLOWN — 8", #305, 1990–1992 only, Americana Series, has painted face (Wendy) 75.00
    BABY — 8", #464-1955, has painted face (Wendy Ann) . . . . 1,200.00 up
    BOBO — 8" h.p., #310, 1991–1992 (Wendy Ann) 100.00
    PIERROT — 8", #561, 1956 only (Wendy Ann) . . . . 1,000.00 up
      14", 1991 only, #1558, white costume with red trim 85.00
    STILTS — 8" #320, 1992–1993, doll on stilts 100.00
COCA COLA CARHOP — 10", #17400, 1997–1999, roller skates 115.00
COCA COLA CELEBRATES AMERICAN AVIATION — 10", #17380, 1998–1999 . . . . 175.00
COCA COLA FANTASY — 10", #31210 – white, #31213 – black, 1997 – 1998 . . . . 155.00
COCA COLA NOSTALGIA — 16", #17490, 1999, white lace dress 220.00
COCA COLA VICTORIAN CALENDAR DOLL — 10", #17360, 1998–1999 . . . . 165.00
COCA COLA WINTER FUN WENDY — 8", #17370, 1999, red ski outfit 100.00
COCO — 21" plastic/vinyl, 1966, in various clothes (other than Portrait) . . . . 2,000.00 up
  In sheath style ballgown . . . . 2,200.00 up
    14", #1558, 1991–1992, Classic Series (Mary Ann) 85.00
    10", #1140, 1989–1992, Portrette, dressed in all black (Cissette) 85.00
    16", #31240, 1997 – 1998, travel wardrobe and dog, Cleo 450.00
    16", #22400, 1998, Belle Epoque, includes houndstooth and glitter gown outfits 325.00
COLLECTOR PIN SERIES — 1999, 2½" polyresin miniature doll 10.00
COLLECTORS UNITED — (see Special Events/Exclusives)
COLLEEN — 10", #1121, 1988 only, Portrette, in green (Cissette) 85.00
COLONIAL — 7" compo., 1937–1938 (Tiny Betty) 300.00
    9" compo., 1936–1939 (Little Betty) 300.00
    8" h.p., BKW, #389, #789, 1962–1964 (Wendy Ann) 325.00
COLUMBIAN SAILOR — (see U.F.D.C. under Special Events/Exclusives)
COLUMBINE — 8", #14575-1995, Nutcracker Series 65.00
COLUMBUS, CHRISTOPHER — 8" h.p., #328, 1992 only, Americana Series 125.00
COMEDIENNE — 10", #20120, clown, 1996 Cirque du Soleil Series 85.00
CONFEDERATE OFFICER — 12", 1990–1991, Scarlett Series (Nancy Drew) 80.00
    8" h.p., 1991–1992, Scarlett Series (see Ashley)

C

Curly Locks, 8", #421 (Wendy).
Made 1987 – 1988 only.

CONGRATULATIONS — 8" h.p., #21180, 1998 (Maggie),
    pink dress balloons. 80.00
COOKIE — 19" compo./cloth, 1938–1940,
    must be in excellent condition 650.00
COOLIDGE, GRACE — 14", 1989–1990, 6th set Presidents'
    Ladies/First Ladies Series (Louisa) 125.00
COPPERTONE BEACH SET — 8", #12110, 1998–1999, bikini,
    umbrella, suntan lotion 140.00
CORAL AND LEOPARD TRAVEL ENSEMBLE — 10",
    #22180, 1997. . . . . 115.00
CORNELIA — Cloth & felt, 1930s . . . . 700.00 up
    21", #2191, 1972, Portrait, dressed in pink
      with full cape (Jacqueline). 450.00
    #2191, 1973, pink with ¾ length jacket. 400.00
    #2296, 1974, blue with black trim 375.00
    #2290, 1975, rose red with black trim and hat 350.00
    #2293, 1976, pink with black trim and hat 350.00
    #2212, 1978, blue with full cape 325.00
COSSACK — 8" h.p. #511, 1989–1991 (Wendy Ann). 70.00
COUNTRY CHRISTMAS — 14", #1543, 1991–1992 only,
    Classic Series (Mary Ann) 150.00
COUNTRY COUSINS — 10" cloth, 1940s. 575.00
    26" cloth, 1940s 650.00
    30" cloth, 1940s 750.00
    16½", 1958, mint (Marybel) 375.00
COUNTRY FAIR — (see Wendy Loves)
COURTNEY AND FRIENDS —
    (see Madame Alexander Doll Company under Special Events/Exclusives)
COUSIN GRACE — 8" h.p., BKW, #432, 1957 only (Wendy Ann) . . . . 1,900.00 up
COUSIN KAREN — 8" h.p., BKW, #620, 1956 only (Wendy Ann) . . . . 1,600.00 up
COUSIN MARIE & MARY — 8" h.p. (Marie - #465; Mary - #462) 1963 only (Wendy Ann) . . . . 1,000.00 each
COWARDLY LION — 8", #431, 1993, Storybook Series #140431-1994–1996, #13220-1997–1999 . . . . 70.00
COWBOY — 8" h.p., BK, #732, 1967–1969, Americana Series (Wendy Ann) 425.00
    8", 1987 (see M.A.D.C. under Special Events/Exclusives)
COWGIRL — 8" h.p., BK, #724, 1967–1970, Americana/Storybook Series (Wendy Ann) 400.00
    10", #1132, 1990–1991, Portrette, white/red outfit (Cissette) 75.00
CRETE — 8" straight leg, #529, 1987 only 70.00
CROATIA — 8", h.p., #110543, 1994 (Wendy Ann) 70.00
CROCKETT, DAVY, BOY OR GIRL — 8" h.p., 1955 only (Boy - #446; Girl - #443) (Wendy Ann) . . . . 700.00 up
CRY DOLLY — 14–16" vinyl, 1953, 12-piece layette 225.00
    14", 16", 19" in swimsuit 100.00–175.00
    16–19" all vinyl, dress or rompers 150.00–225.00
CUBA — 8", #11548, 1995 only, has round brown face 65.00
CUDDLY — 10½" cloth, 1942–1944 . . . . 375.00
    17" cloth, 1942–1944 . . . . 400.00
CUPID — 8", #13860, 1998–1999, (Maggie), white costume, bow, arrow 80.00
CURLY LOCKS — 8" h.p., #472, 1955 only (Wendy Ann) . . . . 850.00 up
    8" straight leg, #421, 1987–1988, Storybook Series, 1997 (Wendy Ann) 85.00
CUTE LITTLE BABY — 14", 1994–1995, doll only . . . . 100.00   With layette and basket. . . 250.00
CYNTHIA — 15" h.p., 1952 only (black "Margaret") . . . . 850.00 up
    18", 1952 only . . . . 850.00 up
    23", 1952 only 1,200.00
CYRANO — 8" h.p., #140505, 1994 only, Storyland Series (Pinocchio). 75.00
CZARINA ALEXANDRA — 8", #12620, 1999, blue satin and gold 80.00
CZECHOSLOVAKIA — 7" compo., 1935–1937 (Tiny Betty) 300.00
    8" h.p., BK, #764, 1972 (Wendy Ann) 100.00
    Straight leg, #0764, #564, 1973–1975, marked "Alex" 65.00

Straight leg, #536, 1976–1987, marked "Alexander"..55.00

8", #536, 1985–1987 ....55.00

8", #521, reintroduced 1992–1993 only (Wendy Ann)..55.00

D

•••••••••••••• PLEASE READ "WHAT IS A PRICE GUIDE?" FOR ADDITIONAL INFORMATION ••••••••••••••

DAFFY DOWN DILLY — 8" straight legs, #429, 1986 only, Storybook Series (Wendy Ann or Maggie) 85.00

DAHL, ARLENE (PINK CHAMPAGNE) — 18" h.p., 1950–1951, red wig, lavender gown (Maggie)   mint ...5,500.00 up

DAISY — 10", #1110, 1987–1989, Portrette series, white lace over yellow (Cissette) 75.00

DAISY RESORT CISSETTE ENSEMBLE — 10", #22380, 1998, silk, linen outfit, chair 160.00

DANISH — 7" compo., 1937–1941 (Tiny Betty) 325.00

    9" compo., 1938–1940 (Little Betty) ,,350.00

DARE, VIRGINIA — 9" compo., 1940–1941 (Little Betty) 450.00

DARLENE — 18" cloth/vinyl, 1991–1992 ....100.00

DAVID AND DIANA — 8" (see FAO Schwarz under Special Events/Exclusives)

DAVID COPPERFIELD — 7" compo., 1936–1938 (Tiny Betty) 350.00

    14" compo., 1938 only (Wendy Ann) 725.00

    16" cloth, early 1930s, Dicken's character ....800.00 up

DAVID, THE LITTLE RABBI — 8" (see Celia's Dolls under Special Events/Exclusives)

DAVID QUACK-A-FIELD OR TWISTAIL — Cloth/felt, 1930s ....700.00 up

DAY OF WEEK DOLLS — 7", 1935–1940 (Tiny Betty) ....350.00 each

    9–11" compo., 1936–1938 (Little Betty) ....375.00 each

    13" compo., 1939 (Wendy Ann) 425.00

DEAR AMERICA SERIES

    ABIGAIL JANE STEWART — 1999, 18", blue print dress 80.00

    CATHERINE CAREY LOGAN — 1999, 18", Pilgrim costume 80.00

    MARGARET ANN BRADY — 1999, 18", pink dress 80.00

    REMEMBER PATIENCE WHIPPLE — 1999, 18", red vest, skirt 80.00

DEAREST — 12" vinyl baby, 1962–1964 ....150.00

DEBRA (DEBORAH) — 21", 1949–1951, Portrette, ballerina with extra make-up (Margaret) ....5,000.00 up

    21", 1949–1951, bride with five-piece

        layered bustle in back ....5,000.00 up

DEBUTANTE — 18" h.p., 1953 only

(Maggie) ....1,250.00 up

DECEMBER — 14", #1528, 1989 only,

Classic Series (Mary Ann) 100.00

DEFOE, DR. ALLEN — 14–15" compo.,

1937–1939 ....1,600.00 up

DEGAS — 21" compo., 1945–1946,

Portrait (Wendy Ann) ....2,250.00 up

DEGAS BALLERINA (THE STAR) — 10", #13910,

1998–1999, (Cissette), white tutu 95.00

DEGAS "DANCE LESSON" — 14"

#241598, 1994 ....95.00

DEGAS GIRL — 14", #1475 (#1575 from 1974),

1967–1987 (20 year production), Portrait

Children and Fine Arts Series

(Mary Ann) 75.00

DELILAH — 8" h.p., #14583, 1995 only,

Bible Series 100.00

DENMARK — 10" h.p., 1962–1963

(Cissette) 650.00

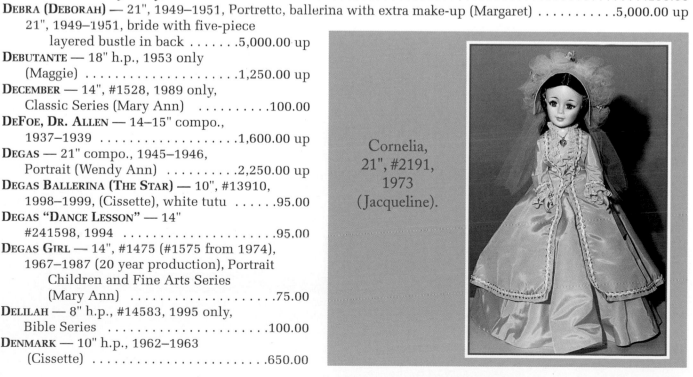

Cornelia,
21", #2191,
1973
(Jacqueline).

8" h.p., BK, #769, 1970–1972 (Wendy Ann) 100.00
8" h.p., straight leg, #0769-569, 1973–1975, marked "Alex" (Wendy) 75.00
8" h.p., straight leg, #546, 1976–1989, marked "Alexander" (1985–1987 white face) (Wendy) 65.00
8" reintroduced, #519, 1991 only (Wendy Ann) 55.00
DESERT STORM — (see Welcome Home)
DIANA — 14", 1993–1994, Anne of Green Gables Series, trunk and wardrobe 275.00
   Tea dress, came with tea set 1993 only 150.00
   Sunday Social 8" #260417, 1994-1995 (Wendy Ann) 100.00
   Sunday Social 14" #261503, 1994 . . . . .125.00
DIAMOND LIL — 10" (see M.A.D.C. under Special Events/Exclusives)
DICKINSON, EMILY — 14", #1587, 1989 only, Classic Series (Mary Ann) .100.00
DICKSIE & DUCKSIE — Cloth/felt, 1930s . . . . .700.00 up
DILLY DALLY SALLY — 7" compo., 1937–1942 (Tiny Betty) 300.00
   9" compo., 1938–1939 (Little Betty) 325.00
DING DONG BELL — 7" compo., 1937–1942 (Tiny Betty) 325.00
DINNER AT EIGHT — 10", #1127, 1989–1991, Portrette, black/white dress (Cissette) 75.00
DINOSAUR — 8" h.p., #343, 1993–1994, Americana Series 65.00
DION, CELINE — 10", 1999, (Cissette), long gown, heart necklace 124.00
DIONNE QUINTS — Original mint or very slight craze.
   Each has own color: Yvonne–pink, Annette–yellow, Cecile–green, Emilie–lavender, Marie–blue
   20" compo. toddlers, 1938–1939 . . . . .700.00 each 4,200.00 set
   19" compo. toddlers, 1936–1938 . . . . .700.00 each 4,200.00 set
   16–17" compo. toddlers, 1937–1939 . . . . .650.00 each 3,600.00 set
   14" compo. toddlers, 1937–1938 . . . . .500.00 each 2,500.00 set
   11" compo. toddlers, 1937–1938, wigs & sleep eyes . . . . .400.00 each 2,200.00 set
   11" compo. toddlers, 1937–1938, molded hair & sleep eyes . . . . .400.00 each 2,200.00 set
   11" compo. babies, 1936, wigs & sleep eyes . . . . .400.00 each 2,200.00 set
   11" compo. babies, 1936, molded hair & sleep eyes . . . . .400.00 each 2,200.00 set
   8" compo. toddlers, 1935–1939, molded hair or wigs & painted eyes . . . . . . .275.00 each 1,300.00 set
   8" compo. babies, 1935–1939, molded hair or wigs & painted eyes . . . . .300.00 each 1,400.00 set
   14" cloth/compo., 1938 . . . . .475.00 each 3,100.00 set
   17" cloth/compo., 1938 . . . . .575.00 each 3,600.00 set
   22" cloth/compo., 1936–1937 . . . . 750.00 each
   24" all cloth, 1935–1936, must be mint . . . . .1,200.00 each
   16" all cloth, 1935–1936, must be mint . . . . .900.00 up

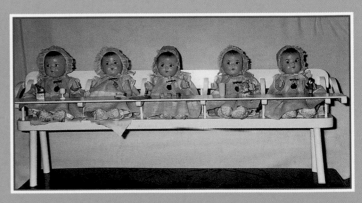

Dominican Republic, 8", #544 (Wendy).
Made from 1986 – 1988 only.

Dionne Quints, 7½", 1936, composition, painted eyes. (High chair not original.)

8" h.p., 1998, 75th Anniversary Set with carousel,
    #12230 . . . . .500.00
8" Yvonne, Marie, Annette, Cecile, Emilie, 1998 . . .85.00 each
DIONNE FURNITURE — (NO DOLLS)
    Scooter, holds 5 . . . . .300.00 up
    Basket case, holds 5 . . . . .225.00
    Divided high chair, holds 5 . . . . .250.00up
    Table and chairs, 5 piece set 400.00
    Ferris wheel, holds 5 .400.00 up
    Bath/shower . . . . .250.00 up
    Wagon, holds 5 . . . . .400.00 up
    Playpen, holds 5 . . . . .250.00 up
    Crib, holds 5 . . . . .250.00 up
    Tricycle . . . . .125.00 each
    Merry-go-round, holds 5 . . . . .350.00 up
    High chair for 1 . . . . .100.00
DISNEY — (see Special Events/Exclusives)
DOGS — (see Poodles)
DOLL FINDERS — (see Special Events/Exclusives)
DOLLS OF THE MONTH — 7–8" compo., 1937–1939, Birthday Dolls
    (Tiny Betty) 350.00
DOLLS 'N BEARLAND — (see Special Events/Exclusives)
DOLLY — 8", #436, 1988–1989, Storybook Series
    (Wendy Ann), 1997 . . . . .90.00
DOLLY DEARS — (see Special Events/Exclusives)
DOLLY DRYPER — 11" vinyl, 1952 only, 7-piece layette 300.00
DOLLY LEVI (MATCHMAKER) — 10" Portrette, 1994 only 75.00
DOMINICAN REPUBLIC — 8" straight leg, #544, 1986–1988 (1985–1986 white face) 70.00
DORMOUSE — 8", #13090, 1998–1999, mouse in sugar bowl w/spoon 95.00
DOROTHY — 14", #1532, 1990–1993, all blue/white check dress and solid blue pinafore (Mary Ann) 95.00
    8" h.p., #464, 1991–1993, #140464, 1994–1995, blue/white check, white bodice (Wendy Ann) 65.00
    8" h.p., emerald green dress special, mid-year special (see Madame Alexander Doll Co. under Special Events/Exclusives)
    8" h.p., #13200, 1997–1999, blue check dress, basket with Toto 60.00
    14" plastic/vinyl, #87007, 1996 . . . . .125.00
DOTTIE DUMBUNNIE — Cloth/felt, 1930s . . . . .800.00 up
DRESSED FOR OPERA — 18" h.p., 1953 only (Margaret) . . . . .1,800.00 up
DRESSED LIKE DADDY — 8", #17002, 1996, white or black 75.00
DRESSED LIKE MOMMY — 8", #17001, 1996 – 1998, white or black 75.00
DRUCILLA — (see M.A.D.C. under Special Events/Exclusives)
DRUM MAJORETTE — (see Majorette)
DUCHESS, THE — 8", #14613, 1996, Alice in Wonderland series 75.00
DUCHESS ELIZA, THE — 10", #20114, 1996 classics 115.00
DUDE RANCH — 8" h.p., #449, 1955 only (Wendy Ann) . . . . .700.00 up
DUDLEY DO-RIGHT AND NELL — 8", #15140, 1999, Dudley in Monty outfit (Maggie), Nell (Wendy)
    includes rope, train track, and backdrop 180.00
DUMPLIN' BABY — 20–23½", 1957–1958 . . . . .185.00
DUTCH — 7" compo., 1935–1939 (Tiny Betty) 300.00
    9" compo boy or girl, 1936–1941 . . . . .325.00
    8" h.p., BKW, #777, 1964, boy* (Wendy) 150.00
    BK, #777, #0777, 1965–1972 . . . . .125.00
    8" h.p., straight leg, #777, *0777, 1972–1973, marked "Alex" .75.00
    8" h.p., BKW, #391-791, 1961–1964, girl* 150.00
    8" h.p. BK, #791, 1965–1972 . . . . .125.00
    8" BKW, #791, 1964 only (Maggie smile face) 150.00
DUTCH LULLABY — 8", #499, 1993, #140499, 1994, Wynkin, Blynkin & Nod, in wooden shoe. 200.00

* **BOTH BECAME NETHERLANDS IN 1974.**

Dolly, 8", #436 (Wendy). Made 1988 – 1989 only. Storyland Series.

·········· PLEASE READ "WHAT IS A PRICE GUIDE?" FOR ADDITIONAL INFORMATION ··········

EASTER — 8", h.p. #21020, 1998, hat with bunny ears, floral dress 70.00

EASTER BONNET — 14", #1562, 1992 (Louisa/Jennifer) 150.00
    8" h.p., #10383–10385, 1995-1996, three hair colors, Special Occasions Series 65.00
    8", h.p., #10401, 1996, African-American 65.00

EASTER BUNNY 8" (see Child at Heart under Special Events/Exclusives)

EASTER DOLL 8" h.p., 1968 only, special for West Coast, in yellow dress (Wendy Ann) . . . . .1,200.00 up
    7½", SLNW, #361, 1953, organdy dress, doll carries basket with chicken . . . . .925.00 up
    14" plastic/vinyl, 1968 only (Mary Ann) . . . . .600.00 up

EASTER OF YESTERDAY — 1995 (see C.U. under Special Events/Exclusives)

EASTER SUNDAY — 8" h.p., #340 or #340-1, 1993 only, Americana Series, black or white doll 70.00
    8", #21510 (white), #21513 (black), 1998–1999, yellow print dress, straw hat, basket 90.00

EBONY AND IVORY HOUNDSTOOTH SUIT — 10", #22190, 1997 – 1998 . . . . .125.00

ECUADOR — 8" h.p., BK & BKW, #878, 1963–1966 (Wendy Ann) 350.00

EDITH, THE LONELY DOLL — 16" plastic/vinyl, 1958–1959 (Mary-Bel) 375.00
    22", 1958–1959 . . . . .400.00
    8" h.p., #850, 1958 only (Wendy Ann) . . . . .750.00 up

EDITH WITH GOLDEN HAIR — 18" cloth, 1940s 675.00

EDWARDIAN — 18" h.p., #2001A, 1953 only, pink embossed cotton, Glamour Girl Series (Margaret) . . . . .1,800.00 up
    8" h.p., #0200, 1953 only (Wendy Ann) . . . . .1,000.00 up

EISENHOWER, MAMIE — 14", 1989–1990, 6th set Presidents' Ladies/First Ladies Series (Mary Ann) 125.00

EGYPT — 8" straight leg, #543, 1986–1989 (round brown face) 65.00

EGYPT WITH SARCOPHAGUS — 8", #24110, 1998–1999, Pharaoh costume 105.00

EGYPTIAN — 7–8" compo., 1936–1940 (Tiny Betty) 325.00
    9" compo., 1936–1940 (Little Betty) 350.00

ELAINE — 18" h.p., 1954 only, Me and My Shadow Series, blue organdy dress (Cissy) . . . . .1,600.00 up
    8" h.p., #0035E, 1954 only, matches 18" (Wendy Ann) . . . . .950.00 up

Elise Bride, 17", #1760, 1968 – 1969. Tulle and lace trimmed gown with sequin panels.

ELISE — 16½" h.p./vinyl arms (18", 1963 only), 1957–1964, jointed ankles & knees, good face color
    In street clothes or blouse, slacks & sash . . . . .400.00 up
    In ballgown, formal, or Portrait . . . . .700.00 up
    In riding habit, 1963 (Marybel head) 400.00
    Ballerina, rare yellow tutu, red hair 700.00
    With Marybel head, 1962 only 400.00
    18", 1963 only, with bouffant hairstyle 425.00
    17" h.p./vinyl, 1961–1962, one-piece arms & legs, jointed ankles & knees 275.00
    18" h.p./vinyl, 1963–1964, jointed ankles & knees 325.00
    In riding habit 350.00
    17" plastic/vinyl, 1966 only, street dress 275.00
    17", 1966–1972, in trunk/trousseau . . . . .650.00 up
    17", 1972–1973, Portrait 225.00
    17", 1966, 1976–1977, in formal 225.00
    17", 1966–1987, Bride 175.00
    17", 1966–1991, Ballerina .100.00
    17", 1966–1989, in any discontinued costume . . . .100.00 up
    16", 1997, #22060, Firebird, red and gold tutu 175.00
    16", 1997, #22050, Giselle, aqua tutu, rose tiara 175.00
    16", 1997, #22040, Swan Lake, white tulle tutu 175.00

ELISE/LESLIE — 14", #1560, 1988 only (Mary Ann) 100.00

ELIZA — 14", #1544, 1991 only, Classic Series (Louisa) . . .150.00

ELIZA THE FLOWER GIRL — 10", #20113, 1996 Classics 100.00

EMILY — Cloth/felt, 1930s 600.00

EMPIRE BRIDE — 10", (Cissette), white lace gown (1999) 135.00

EMPRESS ELIZABETH OF AUSTRIA — 10" (see My Doll House under Special Events/Exclusives)
ENCHANTED DOLL HOUSE — (see Special Events/Exclusives)
ENCHANTED EVENING — 21" Portrait, 1991–1992 only, different necklace than shown in catalog (Cissy) 300.00
ENGLAND — 8", #24040, 1997–1999, Beefeater guard outfit 80.00
ENGLISH GUARD — 8" h.p., BK, #764, 1966–1968, Portrait Children Series (Wendy Ann) 350.00
    8", #515, reintroduced 1989–1991, marked "Alexander" (Wendy Ann) 75.00
ENTERTAINING THE TROOPS — 8", #17550, 1999, red outfit, microphone .75.00
ESKIMO — 8" h.p., BK, #723, 1967–1969, Americana Series (Wendy Ann) 375.00
    9" compo., 1936–1939 (Little Betty) 300.00
    With Maggie Mixup face 425.00
ESTONIA — 8" straight leg, #545, 1986–1987 only (Wendy Ann) 80.00
ESTRELLA — 18", h.p. (Maggie), lilac gown, 1953 . . . . .1,200.00 up
EVA LOVELACE — 7" compo., 1935 only (Tiny Betty) 350.00
    Cloth, 1935 only 600.00
EVA PERON — 10", #22030, 1997, white long lace dress (Cissette) 105.00
EVANGELINE — 18" cloth, 1930s . . . . .650.00 up
EVENING STAR — 15", porcelain, black lace over pink satin (1979) 165.00
EVIL SORCERESS — 8", #13610, 1997, long black velvet dress 75.00

F

. . . . PLEASE READ "WHAT IS A PRICE GUIDE?" FOR ADDITIONAL INFORMATION . . . .

FAO SCHWARZ — (see Special Events/Exclusives)
FAIRY GODMOTHER — 14", #1550, #1551, #1568, 1983–1992, Classic Series (Mary Ann, Louisa) 100.00
    Fairy Godmother outfit, 1983, M.A.D.C. (see Special Events/Exclusives)
    10" Portrette, #1156, 1993 only, blue/gold gown (Cissette) 100.00
    10", #14549, 1995 only, purple gown, white wig (Cissette) 85.00
    8", #13430, 1997–1999, dark blue hooded cloak 75.00
FAIRY OF BEAUTY — 8", #13620, 1997–1999, pink tulle gown 75.00
FAIRY OF SONG — 8", #13630, 1997–1999, green tulle gown 75.00
FAIRY OF VIRTUE — 8", #13640, 1997–1999, blue tulle gown 75.00
FAIRY PRINCESS — 7–8" compo., 1940–1943 (Tiny Betty) 350.00
    9" compo., 1939–1941 (Little Betty) 375.00
    11" compo., 1939 only (Wendy Ann) 375.00
    15–18" compo., 1939–1942 (Wendy Ann) 650.00
    21–22" compo., 1939, 1944–1946 (Wendy Ann) 900.00
FAIRY QUEEN — 14½" compo., 1940–1946 (Wendy Ann) 700.00
    18" compo., 1940–1946 (Wendy Ann) 800.00
    14½" h.p., 1948–1950 (Margaret) 750.00
    18" h.p., 1949–1950 (Margaret) 950.00
FAIRY TALES – DUMAS — 9" compo., 1937–1941 (Little Betty) 375.00
FAITH — 8" h.p., #486, 1961 only, Americana Series, plaid jumper/organdy blouse (Wendy Ann) . . . . . . .1,800.00 up
    8" h.p. (see Collectors United under Special Events/Exclusives)
FANTASY — 8", 1990 (see Doll Finders under Special Events/Exclusives)
FANNIE ELIZABETH — 8" (see Belks & Leggett under Special Events/Exclusives)
FARMER'S DAUGHTER — 8", 1991 (see Enchanted Doll House under Special Events/Exclusives)
FASHIONS OF THE CENTURY — 14–18" h.p., 1954–1955 (Margaret, Maggie) . . . . .1,800.00 up
FATHER CHRISTMAS — 8" h.p., #100351 Americana Series 75.00
FATHER OF THE BRIDE — 10", #24623, 1996, white satin wedding gown 110.00
FATHER OF VATICAN CITY, THE — 8", #24190, 1999, gold silk robe 80.00
FIGURINES — 1999, 6", polyresin replica of Alexander dolls 25.00–28.00
FILLMORE, ABIGAIL — 1982–1984, 3rd set Presidents' Ladies/First Ladies Series (Louisa) 125.00
FINDLAY, JANE — 1979–1981, 1st set Presidents' Ladies/First Ladies Series (Mary Ann) 135.00
FINLAND — 8" h.p., BK, #767, 1968–1972 (Wendy Ann) 100.00

8" h.p., straight leg, #0767-567, 1973–1975, marked "Alex" 75.00
8" h.p., straight leg, #567, 1976–1987, marked "Alexander" 60.00
FINNISH — 7" compo., 1935–1937 (Tiny Betty) 300.00
FIRE FIGHTER WENDY — 8", #31270, 1998–1999, yellow coat, red hat, and dog 85.00
FIRST COMMUNION — 8" h.p., #395, 1957 only (Wendy Ann) 650.00
8" h.p., reintroduced 1994, #100347 Americana Series 75.00
8", #10347–10349, 1995, three hair colors, Special Occassions Series 70.00
8", #17012–17015, 1996, black, three hair colors (Wendy Ann) #21100, 1997 – 1998 . . . . .70.00
8", 1999, #21530 (white), #21534 (black), white dress, veil, Bible 75.00
14", #1545, 1991–1992 only, Classics Series (Louisa) 110.00
FIRST DANCE PAIR — 8", 1996 . . . . .200.00
FIRST LADIES — (see Presidents' Ladies)
FIRST MODERN DOLL CLUB — (see Special Events/Exclusives)
FIRST RECITAL — 8", #17024 (white), #17037 (black), lacy dress 60.00
FISCHER QUINTS — 7" h.p./vinyl, 1964 only, one boy and four girls (Little Genius) . . . . .550.00 set
FIVE LITTLE PEPPERS — 13" & 16" compo, 1936 only . . . . .750.00 each
FLAPPER — 10", Portrette, 1988–1991 (Cissette), red dress 75.00
10", #1118, 1988, black dress (all white dress in 1991) (see M.A.D.C. under Special Events/Exclusives)
8", #14105, 1995, three-tiered rose colored dress with matching headband, Nostalgia Series 55.00
FLORA McFLIMSEY — (with and without "e")
9" compo., 1938–1941 (Little Betty) 425.00
22" compo., 1938–1944 (Princess Elizabeth) . . . . .800.00 up
15–16" compo., 1938–1944 (Princess Elizabeth) . . . . .550.00 up
16–17" compo., 1936–1937 (Wendy Ann) . . . . .550.00 up
14" compo., 1938–1944 (Princess Elizabeth) . . . . .500.00 up
12" compo., 1944 only, holds 5" "Nancy Ann" doll, tagged "Margie Ann" (Wendy Ann) . . . . .950.00 up
15" Miss Flora McFlimsey, vinyl head (must have good color), 1953 only (Cissy) . . . . .700.00 up
14", #25502, 1995, tiers of pink, white, and black, Button & Bows Series (Mary Ann) 135.00
FLOWERGIRL — 16"–18" compo., 1939, 1944–1947 (Princess Elizabeth) 550.00
20–24" compo., 1939, 1944–1947 (Princess Elizabeth) . . . . .650.00 up

Funny Maggie, 8", #140506, 1994 – 1995 (Maggie), yarn hair.

15–18" h.p., 1954 only (Cissy) 450.00–650.00
15" h.p., 1954 only (Margaret) 550.00
8" h.p., #602, 1956 (Wendy Ann) . . . . .900.00 up
8" h.p., #334, 1992–1993, Americana Series,
      white doll (Wendy Ann) 75.00
8", #334-1, 1992 only, black doll 65.00
10", #1122, 1988–1990, Portrette, pink dotted Swiss dress
      (Cissette) 85.00
8", #22620, 1999, mauve satin, rose crown 80.00
FORREST — 8", h.p. #10750, 1998, Tyrolean outfit 80.00
FRANCE — 7" compo., 1936–1943 (Tiny Betty) 300.00
9" compo., 1937–1941 (Little Betty) 325.00
8" h.p., BKW, #390, #790, 1961–1965
      (Wendy Ann) 150.00
8" h.p., BK, #790, 1965–1972 . . . . .125.00
8" h.p., straight leg, #0790, #590, 1973–1975,
      marked "Alex" 75.00
8" straight leg, #590, #552, #517, #582, 1976–1993,
      marked "Alexander" (1985–1987) 60.00
1985–1987, #590, #552, ...65.00
8" h.p., reissued 1994–1995, #110538 (Wendy) 65.00
8" h.p., #11557, 1996 International, cancan costume
      (#24020 – 1998) 70.00
FRENCH ARISTOCRAT — 10" Portrette, #1143, 1991–1992 only,
      bright pink/white (Cissette) 125.00
FRENCH FLOWERGIRL — 8" h.p., #610, 1956 only
      (Wendy Ann) . . . . .750.00 up

FRIAR TUCK — 8" h.p., #493, 1989–1991, Storybook Series (Maggie Mixup) 85.00
FRIEDRICH — (see Sound of Music)
FROU-FROU — 40" all cloth, 1951 only, ballerina with yarn hair, dressed in green or lilac . . . . .800.00 up
FUNNY — 18" cloth, 1963–1977 . . . . .75.00
FUNNY MAGGIE — 8" (Maggie) #140506, 1994–1995, Storyland Series, yarn hair 70.00

G

PLEASE READ "WHAT IS A PRICE GUIDE?" FOR ADDITIONAL INFORMATION

GAINSBOROUGH — 20" h.p., 1957, Models Formal Gowns Series, taffeta gown, large picture hat (Cissy) . .1,400.00 up
    #2184, 21" h.p./vinyl arms, 1968, blue with white lace jacket (Jacqueline) 650.00
    #2192, 21", 1972, yellow with full white lace overskirt (Jacqueline) 650.00
    #2192, 21", 1973, pale blue, scallop lace overskirt (Jacqueline) 600.00
    #2211, 21", 1978, pink with full lace overdress (Jacqueline) 450.00
    10" pink gown & hat, 1957 Portrette (Cissette) 675.00
    10", #45201, 1995, pink with lace overlay, Madame's Portfolio Series 110.00
GARDENIA — 10", #22360, 1998 (Cissette), yellow satin long gown 150.00
GARDEN PARTY — 18" h.p., 1953 only (Margaret) . . . . .1,600.00 up
    20" h.p., 1956–1957 (Cissy) . . . . .1,000.00 up
    8" h.p., #488, 1955 only (Wendy Ann) . . . . .1,800.00 up
GARDEN ROSE — 10", (Cissette), #22530, 1999, pink tulle with roses 130.00
GARFIELD, LUCRETIA — 1985–1987, 4th set Presidents' Ladies/First Ladies Series (Louisa) 115.00
GEMINI — 8", #21350, 1998, African American, 2 dolls, yellow outfit 175.00
GEMINI — 8", #21351, 1998, white, 2 dolls 175.00
GENIUS BABY — 21"–30" plastic/vinyl, 1960–1961, has flirty eyes .150.00–250.00
    Little, 8" h.p. head/vinyl, 1956–1962 (see Little Genius)
GEPETTO — 8", #470, 1993, #140478, 1994,
    Storybook Series 70.00
GERANIUM — 9" early vinyl toddler, 1953 only,
    red organdy dress & bonnet 125.00
GERMAN (GERMANY) — 8" h.p., BK, #763, 1966–1972
    (Wendy Ann) 100.00
    8" h.p., straight leg, #0763-563, 1973–1975,
        marked "Alex" 75.00
    10" h.p., 1962–1963 (Cissette) 925.00
    8" straight legs, #563, #535, #506, 1976–1989,
        marked "Alexander" .65.00
    8", 1990–1991, marked "Alexander" 60.00
    8", #535, 1986 . . . . .60.00
    8" h.p., #110542, 1994–1995, outfit in 1994
        Neiman-Marcus trunk set (Maggie) 60.00
GET WELL — 8", h.p. #21090, 1998–1999, red stripe outfit,
    vase of flowers 80.00
GET WELL WISHES — #10363–10365, 1995, 3 hair colors,
    nurse with bear, Special Occasions Series 60.00
GHOST OF CHRISTMAS PAST — 8", #18002, 1996, Dickens,
    long white gown 60.00
GHOST OF CHRISTMAS PRESENT — 14", #18406, 1996,
    Dickens, sold as set only with
        8" Ignorance (boy) and 8" Want (girl) 325.00
GIBSON GIRL — 10" h.p., 1962, eyeshadow (Cissette) . . .800.00 up
    10", 1963, plain blouse with no stripes . . . . . . .800.00 up
    16" cloth, 1930s 850.00

Gibson Girl, 10", #1124 (Cissette).
Made from 1998 – 1990.

G

10", #1124, 1988–1990, Portrette, red and black (Cissette) 75.00
GIDGET — 14" plastic/vinyl, #1415, #1420, #1421, 1966 only (Mary Ann) 275.00
GIGI — 14", #1597, 1986–1987, Classic Series (Mary Ann) 100.00
    14", #87011, 1996, plaid dress, straw hat (Mary Ann) 125.00
    8", h.p., #13990, 1998–1999, pleated plaid dress, straw hat (Maggie) 80.00
GILBERT — 8", #260420, 1994–1995, Anne Green Gables Series 85.00
GIRL ON FLYING TRAPEZE — 40" cloth, 1951 only, dressed in pink satin tutu (sold at FAO Schwarz) 950.00
GISELLE — 16", #22050, 1998, aqua tutu 195.00
GLAMOUR GIRLS — 18" h.p., 1953 only (Margaret, Maggie) ....1,600.00 up
GLINDA, THE GOOD WITCH — 8", #473, 1992–1993, Storyland Series (Wendy Ann) #140473, 1994-1995 ...100.00
    14" plastic/vinyl, #141573, 1994 only 100.00
    10", #13250, 1997–1999, pink tulle and taffeta dress (Cissette) 115.00
GLORIOUS ANGEL — 10½" h.p., #54860 (see Tree Toppers)
GODEY — 21" compo., 1945–1947 (Wendy Ann) white lace over pink satin ....2,700.00 up
    14" h.p., 1950–1951 (Margaret) 1,500.00
    21" h.p., 1951 only, lace ¾ top with long sleeves, pink satin two-tiered skirt (Margaret) ......1,800.00 up
    18" h.p., #2010A, 1953 only, Glamour Girl Series, red gown with gray fur stole (Maggie) 1,600.00
    21" h.p., vinyl straight arms, 1961 only, lavender coat & hat (Cissy) 1,500.00
    21", 1962, bright orange gown, white lace ruffles on bodice 1,500.00
    21", #2153, 1965, dressed in all red, blonde hair (Jacqueline) 800.00
    21" plastic/vinyl, 1966 only, red with black short jacket & hat (Coco) 2,300.00
    21" h.p., vinyl arms, #2172, 1967, dressed in pink & ecru (Jacqueline) 650.00
    #2195, 1969, red with black trim 600.00
    #2195, 1970, pink with burgundy short jacket 375.00
    #2161, 1971, pink, black trim, short jacket 425.00
    #2298, 1977, ecru with red jacket and bonnet 350.00
    8" SLW, #491, 1955 only (Wendy Ann) ....1,400.00 up
    10" h.p., #1172, 1968, dressed in all pink with ecru lace with bows down front (Cissette) 425.00
        #1172, 1969, all yellow with bows down front 450.00
        #1183, 1970, all lace pink dress with natural straw hat 450.00

Godey, 21", #2298, 1977 (Jacqueline). Ecru dress with red jacket and hat.

GODEY BRIDE — 14" h.p., 1950, lace ¾ top over satin gown with long train (Margaret) ....1,000.00 up
    18" h.p., 1950–1951 (Margaret) ....1,400.00 up
    21" porcelain, 1993 (Cissy) 525.00
GODEY GROOM/MAN — 14" h.p., 1950, has curls over ears, wearing black jacket and tan pants (Margaret) ....975.00 up
    18" h.p., 1950–1951 (Margaret) ....1,200.00 up
GODEY LADY — 14" h.p., 1950, green velvet dress with pink/bright orange pleated ruffles, peach/white bodice (Margaret) ....1,000.00 up
    18" h.p., 1950–1951 (Margaret) ....1,500.00 up
GOLDFISH — 8" h.p., #344, Americana Series 1993–1994 ....80.00
GOLD RUSH — 10" h.p., 1963 only (Cissette) 1,600.00
GOLDILOCKS — 18" cloth, 1930s ....875.00 up
    7–8" compo., 1938–1942 (Tiny Betty) 300.00
    18" h.p., 1951 only (Maggie) ....1,300.00 up
    14" plastic/vinyl, #1520, 1978–1979, Classic Series, satin dress (Mary Ann) 115.00
    14", #1520, 1980–1983, blue satin or cotton dress (Mary Ann) 100.00
    14", #1553, 1991 only, Classic Series, long side curls tied with ribbon (Mary Ann) 100.00
    8", #497, 1990–1991 only, Storyland Series (1991 dress in different plaid) (Wendy Ann) 75.00
    8", #140500, 1994–1995, Storyland Series, floral print dress, has bear 75.00
GOLF BOY — 8", 1998, #16402 (Maggie) green coat, checked hat, pants, golf club 75.00

GOLF GIRL — 8", 1998, #16412 (Wendy) ivory sweater, navy skirt, golf club 75.00
GONE WITH THE WIND (SCARLETT) — 14", #1490, #1590, 1969–1986, all white dress/green sash,
   made 17 years without a change (Mary Ann) (dress must be mint) 150.00
GOOD FAIRY — 14" h.p., 1948–1949 (Margaret) . . . . .725.00 up
GOOD LITTLE GIRL — 16" cloth, 1966 only, mate to "Bad Little Girl," wears pink dress 150.00
GOYA — 8" h.p., #314, 1953 only (Wendy Ann) . . . . .1,000.00 up
   21" h.p./vinyl arms, #2183, 1968, multi-tiered pink dress (Jacqueline) 550.00
   21", #2235, 1982–1983, maroon dress with black Spanish lace (Jacqueline) 325.00
GRADUATION — 8" h.p., #399, 1957 only (Wendy Ann) . . . . .850.00 up
   12", 1957 only (Lissy) 800.00
   8", #307, 1990–1991, Americana Series (white doll only) (Wendy Ann) .75.00
   8", #307, #307-1, 1991–1992, Americana Series, white or black doll 70.00
   8", #10307–10309 (black), #10310 (white), 1995, blue robe, Special Occasions Series 70.00
GRAND OLE OPRY BOY — 8", #77005, 1996 Classic 80.00
GRAND OLE OPRY GIRL — 8", #77004, 1996 Classic 80.00
GRANDMA JANE — 14" plastic/vinyl, #1420, 1970–1972 (Mary Ann) 250.00
GRANT, JULIA — 1982–1984, 3rd set Presidents' Ladies/First Ladies Series (Louisa) 125.00
GRAVE, ALICE — 18" cloth, 1930s . . . . .750.00 up
GRAYSON, KATHRYN — 20–21" h.p., 1949 only (Margaret) . . . . .5,500.00 up
GREAT BRITAIN — 8" h.p., #558, 1977–1988 (Wendy Ann) 60.00
GREAT GATSBY PAIR — 10", #15310, 1997, classic characters 180.00
GREECE BOY — 8" h.p., #527, 1992–1993 only (Wendy Ann) 55.00
GREEK BOY — 8" h.p., BK, 1965, & BKW, 1966–1968, #769 (Wendy Ann) 350.00
GREEK GIRL — 8" h.p., BK, #765, 1968–1972 (Wendy Ann) 100.00
   8" h.p., straight leg, #0765, #565, 1973–1975, marked "Alex" 75.00
   8" h.p., straight leg, #565, #527, 1976–1987 (1985–1987), marked "Alexander" 65.00
GRETEL — 7" compo., 1935–1942 (Tiny Betty) 300.00
   9" compo., 1938–1940 (Little Betty) 325.00
   18" h.p., 1948 only (Margaret) . . . . .1,000.00 up
   7½–8" h.p., SLW, #470, 1955 (Wendy Ann) . . . . .400.00 up
   8" h.p., BK, #754, 1966–1972, Storybook Series (Wendy) 100.00
   8" h.p., straight leg, #0754, #454, 1973–1975, marked "Alex" 75.00
   8" h.p., straight leg, #454, 1976–1986, marked "Alexander" 65.00
   8" h.p., #462, 1991–1992 only, Storyland Series, reintroduced doll (Wendy Ann) 65.00
GRETEL BRINKER — 12", 1993 only (Lissy) 150.00
   8", #14650, 1996 . . . . .70.00
GRETL — (see Sound of Music)
GROOM — 18"–21" compo., 1946–1947, mint (Margaret) 975.00
   18–21" h.p., 1949–1951 (Margaret) . . . . .850.00 up
   14–16" h.p., 1949–1951 (Margaret) . . . . .750.00 up
   7½" h.p., SL & SLW, #577, #464, #466, 1953–1955 (Wendy Ann) . . . . .450.00 up
   8" BKW, #577, 1956 . . . . .375.00
   8" BKW, #377, 1957 . . . . .375.00
   8" BKW, #572, 1958 . . . . .375.00
   8" h.p., BKW, #421, #442, 1961–1963 (Wendy Ann) 350.00
   8", #488, #388, reintroduced 1989–1991 only (Wendy Ann) 70.00
   8", #339, 1993, only black pants, peach tie, white jacket 70.00
   8", #17020, 1996, black velvet tails, black pants, pink tie 70.00
   8", #17023, 1996, black velvet tails, etc., black doll 70.00
   8", #21071, 1997–1999, velvet tailcoat, top hat, #21073 — African American (1997–1998) 60.00
GUARDIAN ANGEL — 10", #10602–1995, first in series, 100th Anniversary Special, all pink with white wings 125.00
   10" #10720, 1998, rose print brocade gown, feather wings 125.00
   10", of Harmony, #10691, 1996 . . . . .100.00
   10", of Hope, #10609, 1996 . . . . .100.00
   10", of Love, frosted ivy, #10605, 1996 . . . . .100.00
   10", of Love, heather blue #10607, 1996 . . . . .100.00
   10", of Love, misty rose, #10603, 1996 . . . . .100.00

G

G

10", pink pristine, #10700, 1997–1999, pink tulle dress 115.00
10", #10720, 1999, pink print brocade gown, feather wings 110.00
GUATEMALA — 8", #24180, 1999, red and black outfit 80.00
GUINEVERE — 10", #1146, 1992 only, Portrette, forest green/gold 125.00
8", #13570, 1999, blue dress with white brocade overdress 75.00

H

· · · · · · · · · · · · · · · PLEASE READ "WHAT IS A PRICE GUIDE?" FOR ADDITIONAL INFORMATION · · · · · · · · · · · · · · ·

HALLOWEEN WITCH — 8" (see Collectors United under Special Events/Exclusives)
HAMLET — 12", Romance Series (Nancy Drew) 90.00
12", 1993 only (Lissy) 125.00
HANS BRINKER — 12", 1993 only (Lissy) 150.00
8", #14649, 1996 . . . . .60.00
HANSEL — 7" compo., 1935–1942 (Tiny Betty) 300.00
9" compo., 1938–1940 (Little Betty) 350.00
18" h.p., 1948 only (Margaret) . . . . .800.00 up
8" h.p., SLW, #470, 1955 only (Wendy Ann) . . . . .550.00 up
8" h.p., BK, #753, 1966–1972, Storybook Series (Wendy Ann) 100.00
8" h.p., straight leg, #0753, #543, 1973–1975, marked "Alex" 75.00
8" h.p., straight leg, #543, 1976–1986 (1986 white face), marked "Alexander" 65.00
8" h.p., #461, 1991–1992 only, Storyland Series, reintroduced doll (Wendy Ann) 60.00
HAPPY — 20" cloth/vinyl, 1970 only 225.00
HAPPY BIRTHDAY — 1985 (see M.A.D.C. under Special Events/Exclusives)
8" h.p., #325, #325-1, 1992–1993, Americana Series, black or white doll (Wendy Ann) 65.00
8" h.p., #100325, 1994, white only 65.00
8", #10325–10327, 1995, three hair colors, Special Occasions Series 65.00
8", #17004–17010, 1996, three hair colors, black or white doll (Wendy, Maggie) 65.00
14" plastic/vinyl, #241596, 1994 only 100.00

Hansel, 8". Left: #543, 1983. Right: 1986 (Wendy). Notice the variation in the print on the shirts.

Heidi, 14", plastic/vinyl (Mary Ann). Made from 1969 – 1985 in a variety of print dresses.

8", #21520 (blonde), #21521 (brunette), #21523 (black), pink print dress 70.00
HAPPY BIRTHDAY BILLIE — 8" h.p., #345, #345-1, Americana Series, black or white boy, 1993 only 65.00
HAPPY BIRTHDAY MAGGIE — 8", #21080 – white, #21083 – black, 1997–1998 . . . . .65.00
HAPPY CHANUKAH — 8", #10367, 1996 Holiday, #19630, 1997–1999 . . . . .75.00
HAPPY THE CLOWN — 8", #10414, 1996 Classic Circus 65.00
HARDING, FLORENCE — 1988, 5th set Presidents' Ladies/First Ladies Series (Louisa) 125.00
HARLEQUIN — 8", #14574, 1995, Nutcracker Series 65.00
HARLEY DAVIDSON
   8", h.p., #77002, 1996 (Wendy) Classic American, #17420, 1997 . . . . .100.00
   8", h.p., #77005, 1996 (Billy) Classic American, #17410, 1997 . . . . .100.00
   10", h.p. #77102, 1996, pictured 1996 catalog . . . . .Not Available for Sale
   10", #17440, 1997, Cissette, black leather coat, boots 125.00
   10", #17430, 1997, David, jeans, black leather jacket 125.00
   10", #17390, 1998, Cissette, faux leather halter and skirt and backpack 160.00
HARRISON, CAROLINE — 1985–1987, 4th set Presidents' Ladies/First Ladies Series (Louisa) 125.00
HAWAII — 8", #301, 1990–1991 only, Americana Series (Wendy Ann) 75.00
HAWAIIAN — 8" h.p., BK, #722, 1966–1969, Americana Series (Wendy Ann) 375.00
   7" compo., 1936–1939 (Tiny Betty) 300.00
   9" compo., 1937–1944 (Little Betty) 350.00
HAYES, LUCY — 1985–1987, 4th set Presidents' Ladies/First Ladies Series (Louisa) 125.00
HEATHER — 18" cloth/vinyl, 1990 only 100.00
     8", h.p., #10760, 1998, Tyrolean outfit with basket 90.00
HEIDI — 7" compo., 1938–1939 (Tiny Betty) 300.00
   8" h.p., #460, 1991–1992, Storyland Series (Maggie) 75.00
   14" plastic/vinyl, #1480, #1580, #1581, 1969–1985 (16 year production), Classic Series (Mary Ann) . . .85.00
   14", #1581, 1986–1988, solid green dress, floral apron 85.00
   14", #25503, 1995, Ribbons & Bows Series (not on order sheet) . . . . Not Available
   8", h.p., #15100, 1998–1999, green dress, lace apron, straw hat, goat 80.00
HELLO BABY — 22", 1962 only 175.00
HENIE, SONJA — 13–15" compo., 1939–1942 . . . . .600.00
   7" compo., 1939–1942 (Tiny Betty) 425.00
   9" compo., 1940–1941 (Little Betty) 575.00
   11" compo. (Wendy Ann) 550.00
   14" compo. 675.00
   14" in case/wardrobe . . . . .1,800.00 up
   17–18" compo. 950.00
   20–23" compo. 1,200.00
   13–14" compo., jointed waist 750.00
   15–18" h.p./vinyl, 1951 only, no extra joints, must have good face color (Madeline) 750.00
HER FIRST DAY AT SCHOOL — (see Wendy Loves Series)
HER LADY AND CHILD (THUMBELINA) — 21" porcelain, 8" h.p., #010, 1992–1994, limited to 2,500 . . . . .500.00
HER SUNDAY BEST — (see Wendy Loves Series)
HIAWATHA — 8" h.p., #720, 1967–1969, Americana Series (Wendy Ann) 375.00
   7" compo. (Tiny Betty) 300.00
   18" cloth, early 1930s 800.00
HICKORY DICKORY DOCK — 8", #11650, 1998–1999, clock costume 85.00
HIGHLAND FLING — 8" h.p., #484, 1955 only (Wendy Ann) 750.00
HOLIDAY ON ICE — 8" h.p., #319, 1992–1993 only, red with white fur hat and muff,
   some tagged Christmas on Ice 125.00
HOLLAND — 7" compo., 1936–1943 (Tiny Betty) 300.00
HOLLY — 10", #1135, 1990–1991, Portrette, white/red roses (Cissette) 100.00
HOLLYWOOD TRUNK SET — 8", #15340, 1997 . . . . .250.00
HOMECOMING — 8", 1993 (see M.A.D.C. under Special Events/Exclusives)
HOME FOR HOLIDAYS — 14", #24606, 1995, Christmas Series 105.00
HONEYBEA — 12" vinyl, 1963 only 175.00
HONEYETTE BABY — 16" compo./cloth, 1941–1942 . . . . .225.00
   7" compo., 1934–1937, little girl dress (Tiny Betty) 275.00

HONEYBUN — 18–19", 1951–1952 only 200.00

23–26" 300.00

HONEYMOON IN NEW ORLEANS — 8" (see Scarlett)

HOOVER, LOU — 14", 1989–1990, 6th set Presidents' Ladies/First Ladies Series (Mary Ann) 125.00

HOPE — 8" (see Collectors United under Special Events/Exclusives)

HOWDY DOODY TIME, IT'S — 8", #15230, 1999, marionette 100.00

HUCKLEBERRY FINN — 8" h.p., #490, 1989–1991 only, Storybook Series (Wendy Ann) 85.00

HUG ME PETS — #76001–76007, plush animal bodies, huggums face 60.00

HUGGUMS, BIG — 25", 1963–1979, boy or girl 100.00

HUGGUMS, LITTLE — 14", 1986 only, molded hair 50.00

12", 1963–1995, molded hair, available in 7–10 outfits (first black version available in 1995) 50.00

12", 1963–1982, 1988, rooted hair 40.00

1991, special outfits (see Imaginarium Shop under Special Events/Exclusives)

1996 – 1998, variety of outfits . . . . .40.00 up

12", #29700, 1998, 75th Anniversary Huggums, white dress with flowers .75.00

HUGGUMS, LIVELY — 25", 1963 only, knob makes limbs and head move 150.00

HUGGUMS MAN IN THE MOON MOBILE — #14700, 8" boy, star costume, cloth moon, star mobiles 70.00

HULDA — 18" h.p., 1949 only, lamb's wool wig black doll (Margaret) .1,900.00 up

14" h.p., 1948–1949, lamb's wool wig, black doll . . . . .1,275.00 up

HUMPTY DUMPTY — 8", #13060, 1997 – 1998, plaid tailcoat, brick wall 70.00

HUNGARIAN (HUNGARY) — 8" h.p., BKW, #397, #797, 1962–1965 (Wendy Ann) 150.00

BK, #397, with metal crown 150.00

BK, #797, 1965–1972 . . . . .100.00

8" h.p., straight leg, #0797, #597, 1973–1976, marked "Alex" 70.00

8" h.p., straight leg, #597, 1976–1986, marked "Alexander" 60.00

8" h.p., #522, reintroduced 1992–1993 only (Wendy) 60.00

8", #11547, 1995 only 60.00

HYACINTH — 9" early vinyl toddler, 1953 only, blue dress & bonnet 150.00

Hungarian, 8", Wendy. Left: Bk with metal crown, 1970. Right: #597, 1982.

Israel, 8", Wendy. Made from 1965 to 1989 with changes in ribbons and variation in blue of skirt. Made as BKW, BK, and SLNW.

·············· PLEASE READ "WHAT IS A PRICE GUIDE?" FOR ADDITIONAL INFORMATION ··············

IBIZA — 8", #510, 1989 only (Wendy Ann) 80.00
ICE CAPADES — 1950s (Cissy) ....1,400.00 up
   1960s (Jacqueline) ....1,600.00 up
ICE SKATER — 8" h.p., BK & BKW, #555, 1955–1956 (Wendy Ann) ....700.00 up
   8", #303, 1990–1991 only, Americana Series, purple/silver (Wendy Ann) 75.00
   8", #16371, 1997, boy, brocade vest, black pants 65.00
   8", #16361, 1997 – 1998, girl, pink knit and silver outfit.................................65.00
ICELAND — 10", 1962–1963 (Cissette) ....750.00 up
IGNORANCE — 8", #18406 (see Ghost of Christmas Present) (sold as set)
I LOVE YOU — 8", #10386–10388, 1995, three hair colors, Special Occasions Series 60.00
I. MAGNIN — (see Special Events/Exclusives)
IMAGINARIUM SHOP — (see Special Events/Exclusives)
INDIA — 8" h.p., BKW, #775, 1965 (Wendy Ann) 150.00
   8" h.p., BK, #775, 1965–1972 (Wendy) 100.00
   8" h.p., #775, BK & BKW, white 100.00
   8" h.p., straight leg, #0775, #575, 1973–1975, marked "Alex" 70.00
   8" h.p., straight leg, #575, #549, 1976–1988, marked "Alexander" (1985–1987) 60.00
   8" h.p., straight leg, #11563, 1996 International, #24030, 1997 ....65.00
INDIAN BOY* — 8" h.p., BK, #720, 1966 only, Americana Series (Wendy Ann) 500.00
INDIAN GIRL* — 8" h.p., BK, #721, 1966 only, Americana Series (Wendy Ann) 450.00
INDONESIA — 8" h.p., BK, #779, 1970–1972 (Wendy) 100.00
   8" h.p., straight leg, #779, #0779, #579, 1972–1975, marked "Alex" 75.00
   8" h.p., straight leg, #579, 1976–1988, marked "Alexander" 60.00
   8" BK, with Maggie Mixup face 175.00
INGALLS, LAURA — 14", #1531, 1989–1991, Classic Series, burnt orange dress/blue pinafore (Mary Ann) ..100.00
   14", #24621, 1995, green with rose floral, Favorite Books Series (Mary Ann) 105.00
INGRES — 14" plastic/vinyl, #1567, 1987 only, Fine Arts Series (Mary Ann) 90.00
IRIS — 10" h.p., #1112, 1987–1988, pale blue (Cissette) 90.00
IRISH (IRELAND) — 8" h.p., BKW, #778, 1965 only (Wendy Ann) 125.00
   8" BK, #778, 1966–1972, long gown 100.00
   8" straight leg, #0778, #578, 1973–1975, marked "ALEX," long gown 75.00
   8" straight leg, #578, #551, 1976–1985, marked "Alexander" 65.00
   8" straight leg, #551, 1985–1987, short dress 60.00
   8" straight leg, #551, 1987–1993, marked "Alexander," short dress (Maggie) 60.00
   8" h.p., #100541, re-issued 1994 only, green skirt with white top 60.00
   8" h.p., #17028, 1996 International, Leprechaun outfit, #21000, 1997–1999 ....60.00
IRISH LASS — 8", #11555, 1995 only 60.00
ISOLDE — 14", #1413, 1985–1986 only, Opera Series (Mary Ann) 90.00
ISRAEL — 8" h.p., BK, #768, 1965–1972 (Wendy Ann) 100.00
   8" h.p., straight leg, #0768, 1973–1975, marked "Alex" 75.00
   8" h.p., straight leg, #568, 1976–1989, marked "Alexander" 65.00
ITALY — 8" h.p., BKW, #393, 1961–1965 (Wendy Ann) 125.00
   8" h.p., BK, #793, 1965–1972 ....100.00
   8" h.p., straight leg, #0793, #593, 1973–1975, marked "ALEX" 70.00
   #593, 1985 ....65.00
   8" straight leg, #593, #553, #524, 1976–1994 (#110524), marked "Alexander" 65.00
   8", #11549, 1995 only 65.00
   8", #24050, 1997 – 1998, gondolier outfit, with decorated oar 70.00
* BECAME HIAWATHA AND POCAHONTAS IN 1967.

PLEASE READ "WHAT IS A PRICE GUIDE?" FOR ADDITIONAL INFORMATION

JABBERWOCKY — 8", #13580, 1999, gold costume, comes with brick tower 75.00

JACK & JILL — 7" compo., 1938–1943 (Tiny Betty) . . . . 275.00 each
    9" compo., 1939 only (Little Betty) · 325.00 each
    8" straight leg (Jack - #455, #457. Jill - #456, #458), 1987–1992, Storybook Series (Maggie) . . . . 65.00 each
    8" straight leg, sold as set, #14626, 1996 (Wendy) 105.00

JACK BE NIMBLE — 8" (see Dolly Dears under Special Events/Exclusives)

JACKIE — 10", #45200, 1995, Madame's Portfolio Series, pink suit 85.00
    10" h.p., #20115, 1996, wedding gown, Classic American 105.00
    21", #17450, 1997, 3 outfits, 3 pieces luggage, jewelry, etc. 630.00
    10", #17460, 1997 – 1998, pink luncheon suit 105.00
    10", #17470, 1998, opera coat, evening dress 120.00
    10", #17480, 1998, beaded cocktail dress 120.00

JACKIE AND JOHN — 10", #20117, 1996, limited edition . . . . .210.00 set

JACKSON, SARAH — 1979–1981, 2nd set Presidents' Ladies/First Ladies Series (Louisa) 125.00

JACQUELINE IN RIDING HABIT — 21" h.p./vinyl arms, 1961–1962, street dress or suit, pillbox hat . . . . .850.00 up
    In sheath dress and hat or slacks and top 650.00
    In gown from cover of 1962 catalog 950.00
    Ballgown other than 1962 catalog cover 850.00
    10" h.p., 1962 only (Cissette) 700.00

JACQUELINE — 1962, 1966–1967, exclusive in trunk with wardrobe . . . . .1,800.00 up

JAMAICA — 8" straight leg, #542, 1986–1988 (round brown face) 80.00

JANIE — 12" toddler, #1156, 1964–1966 only 275.00
    Ballerina, 1965 only 350.00
    14" baby, 1972–1973 . . . . .65.00

Jacqueline, 21", h.p./vinyl, 1961.
In original riding habit and boots.

    20" baby, 1972–1973 . . . . .85.00

JAPAN — 8" h.p., BK, #770, 1968–1972 (Wendy) 100.00
    8" h.p., straight leg,#0770, #570, 1973–1975,
      marked "Alex" 75.00
    8" h.p., straight leg, #570, 1976–1986,
      marked "Alexander" 65.00
    8", #570, 1987–1991 (Maggie) 65.00
    8" BK, #770, 1960s (Maggie Mixup) 225.00
    8" h.p., #526, reintroduced 1992–1993 only,
      white face (Wendy Ann) 65.00

JASMINE — 10", #1113, 1987–1988,
    Portrette, burnt orange (Cissette), 1997 . . . . .85.00

JEANNIE WALKER — 13–14" compo., 1940s, unique jointed legs,
    excellent face color, mint condition . . . . . . .675.00 up
    18" compo., 1940s . . . . .725.00 up

JENNIFER'S TRUNK SET — 14" doll, #1599, 1990 only 250.00

JESSICA — 18" cloth/vinyl, 1990 only 150.00

JINGLES THE JUGGLER — 8", #10404, 1996, jester's outfit . . .75.00

JO — (see Little Women)

JO GOES TO NEW YORK — 8", #14522, 1995 only,
    trunk set, Little Women Series . . . . .225.00 set

JOANIE — 36" plastic/vinyl, 1960–1961, allow more for flirty eyes
    36", 1960, nurse dressed in all white
      with black band on cap . . . . .475.00 up
    36", 1961, nurse in colored uniform,
      all white pinafore and cap . . . . .425.00 up

JOHN — 8", #440, 1993 only, Peter Pan Series,
    wears glasses 75.00

JOHN POWERS MODELS — 14" h.p., 1952 only, must be mint
    (Maggie & Margaret) . . . . .1,650.00 up
    18", 1952 only . . . . .1,900.00 up

JONES, CASEY — 8" h.p., Americana Series, 1991–1992 only
(Wendy Ann) 60.00
JOHNSON, LADY BIRD — 14", 1994 only 125.00
JOLLY OLD SAINT NICK — 16", #19620, 1997 ....190.00
JOSEPH, THE DREAM TELLER — 8", #14580, 1995 only, Bible Series ...85.00
JOSEPHINE — 12", #1335, 1980–1986, Portraits of History (Nancy Drew) 75.00
   21" Portrait, 1994 only 325.00
JOY — 12"
   (see New England Collectors Society under Special Events/Exclusives)
JOY NOEL — 8" (see Spiegel's under Special Events/Exclusives)
JUDY — 21" compo., 1945–1947, pinch pleated flowers at hem
(Wendy Ann) ....3,200.00 up
   21" h.p./vinyl arms, 1962 only (Jacqueline) ....1,800.00 up
JUGO-SLAV — 7" compo., 1935–1937 (Tiny Betty) 225.00
JULIET — 21" compo., 1945–1946, Portrait (Wendy Ann) .....2,500.00 up
   18" compo., 1937–1940 (Wendy Ann) ....1,275.00 up
   8" h.p., #473, 1955 only (Wendy Ann) ....950.00 up
   12" plastic/vinyl, 1978–1987, Portrait Children Series
(Nancy Drew) 65.00
   12", reintroduced 1991–1992, Romance Collection
(Nancy Drew) 85.00
   8" (see Madame Alexander Doll Company under Specials Events/Exclusives)
JUNE BRIDE — 21" compo., 1939, 1946–1947, Portrait Series, embroidered flowers near hem
(Wendy Ann) ....2,500.00 up
JUNE WEDDING — 8" h.p., 1956 (Wendy Ann) 650.00

Jacqueline, 10", 1962, hard plastic (Cissette). Satin gown with stole.

K

•••••••••••••••• PLEASE READ "WHAT IS A PRICE GUIDE?" FOR ADDITIONAL INFORMATION ••••••••••••••••

KAREN — 15–18" h.p., 1948–1949 (Margaret) ....850.00 up
KAREN BALLERINA — 15" compo., 1946–1949 (Margaret) ....900.00 up
   18" compo., 1948–1949 (Margaret) ....1,200.00 up
   18–21", h.p., can be dressed in pink, yellow, blue, white, or lavender ....950.00 up
   15", porcelain, 1999, #90200, remake of 1940s Ballerina 160.00
KATE GREENAWAY — 7" compo., 1938–1943 (Tiny Betty) 350.00
   9" compo., 1936–1939 (Little Betty) 375.00
   16" cloth, 1936–1938 ....900.00
   13", 14", 15" compo., 1938–1943 (Princess Elizabeth) 750.00
   18", 1938–1943 (Wendy Ann/Princess Elizabeth) 800.00
   24", 1938–1943 (Princess Elizabeth) ....900.00 up
   14" vinyl, #1538, 1993 only, Classic Series 100.00
KATHLEEN TODDLER — 23" rigid vinyl, 1959 only 150.00
KATHY — 17"–21" compo., 1939, 1946 (Wendy Ann) 650.00–850.00
   15–18" h.p., 1949–1951, has braids (Maggie) 550.00–700.00
KATHY BABY — 13–15" vinyl, 1954–1956, has rooted or molded hair 75.00–125.00
   11–13" vinyl, 1955–1956, has rooted or molded hair 75.00–125.00
   18–21", 1954–1956, has rooted or molded hair 100.00–150.00
   11" vinyl, 1955–1956, doll has molded hair and comes with trousseau 175.00
   21", 1954 only 150.00
   21" & 25", 1955–1956 ....100.00–175.00
KATHY CRY DOLLY — 11–15" vinyl nurser, 1957–1958 ....75.00–125.00
   18", 21", 25" 100.00–175.00
KATHY TEARS — 11", 15", 17" vinyl, 1959–1962, has closed mouth 75.00–125.00
   19", 23", 26", 1959–1962 ....100.00–175.00
   12", 16", 19" vinyl, 1960–1961 (new face) 75.00–150.00

Kelly, 12" (Lissy), hard plastic, 1959 only, original clothes.

KATIE (BLACK SMARTY) — 12" plastic/vinyl, 1963 only 325.00
    12" (black Janie), #1156, #1155, 1965 only 300.00
    12" h.p., 1962, 100th Anniversary doll for FAO Schwarz
       (Lissy) 1,000.00
KEANE, DORIS — Cloth, 1930s 750.00
    9–11" compo., 1936–1937 (Little Betty) 250.00–300.00
KELLY — 12" h.p., 1959 only (Lissy) 475.00
    15–16", 1958–1959 (Marybel) 325.00
    16", 1959 only, in trunk/wardrobe . . . . .800.00 up
    18", 1958 . . . . .375.00
    22", 1958–1959 . . . . .400.00
    8" h.p., #433, 1959, blue/white dress (Wendy Ann) 575.00
KELLY AND KITTY — 20", #29770, 1999, pink check outfit
    with kitten 135.00
KELLY BLUE GINGHAM — 18", #29100, 1997 – 1998, vinyl 125.00
KELLY BLUE DUPIONNE — 20", #29380, 1998, blue silk dress 160.00
KELLY GOOD MORNING — 20", #29930, 1999, white dress
    trimmed in blue 105.00
KELLY HAPPY BIRTHDAY — 18", #29230, 1997, vinyl 125.00
KELLY'S LITTLE SISTER, KATIE — 12", #29940, 1999, pink plaid dress 55.00
KELLY PINK BUTTERFLY — 20", #29920, 1999,
    pink dress and pinafore 105.00
KELLY PINK DOT TULLE — 18", #29230, 1997, vinyl 125.00
KELLY PINK SNOWFLAKE — 18", #29110, 1997, vinyl 125.00
KELLY TEACHER'S PET — 15", #29760, 1999, plaid dress and hat 75.00
KELLY TEATIME — 15", #29300, 1998, blue dress, straw hat 85.00
KELLY TREE TRIMMING — 18", #29240, 1997, vinyl 125.00
KELLY WHITE FLORAL PARTY — 15", vinyl #29390, 1998–1999 . . . . .105.00
KENNEDY, JACQUELINE — 14", 1989–1990, 6th set Presidents' Ladies/First Ladies Series (Mary Ann) 175.00
KENYA — 8", 1994, outfit tagged, in Neiman-Marcus trunk set
    8", issued 1995 only, same outfit but sold as **NIGERIA** . . . . No Price Available
KING — 21" compo., 1942–1946 , extra makeup, red chest ribbon, gold trimmed cape (Wendy Ann) 2,700.00 up
KING OF HEARTS — 8", #14611, 1996, Alice in Wonderland series 65.00
KITTEN — 14–18" cloth/vinyl, 1962–1963 . . . . .50.00–85.00
    24", 1961 only, has rooted hair 95.00
    20" nurser, 1968 only, has cryer box, doesn't wet 100.00
    20", 1985–1986 only, dressed in pink 90.00
    8", 1998, #29310 Powder Pink or #29423 Sunny 60.00
KITTY BABY — 21" compo., 1941–1942 . . . . .175.00
KITTEN KRIES — 20" cloth/vinyl, 1967 only 100.00
KITTEN, LITTLEST — (see Littlest Kitten)
KITTEN, LIVELY — 14", 18", 24", 1962–1963, knob moves head and limbs 100.00–175.00
KITTEN, MAMA — 18", #402, 1963 only, same as "Lively" but also has cryer box 150.00
KLONDIKE KATE — 10" h.p., 1963 only, Portrette (Cissette) . . . . .1,400.00 up
KNAVE — 8", #13040, 1997 – 1998, brocade suit, large playing card, *5 of Spades* 75.00
KOREA — 8" h.p., BK, #772, 1968–1970 (Wendy) 175.00
    BKW & BK, #772 (Maggie Mixup) 225.00
    #522, reintroduced 1988–1989 (Maggie Mixup) 75.00
KUKLA — 8", #11101, 1995 only, International Folk Tales (Russia) (Wendy) .65.00
KWANZAA CELEBRATION — 10" h.p., #10368, 1996 Holiday 95.00

•••••••••••••••• PLEASE READ "WHAT IS A PRICE GUIDE?" FOR ADDITIONAL INFORMATION ••••••••••••••••

LADY AND HER CHILD — 21" porcelain, 8" h.p., 1993 . . . . .500.00 set
LADY BIRD — 8", #438, 1988–1989, Storybook Series (Maggie) 85.00
LADY HAMILTON — 20" h.p./vinyl arms, 1957 only, Models Formal Gowns Series, picture hat,
    blue gown w/ shoulder shawl effect (Cissy) . . . . .850.00 up
    11" h.p., 1957, pink silk gown, picture hat with roses (Cissette) . . . . .750.00 up
    21", #2182, 1968, beige lace over pink gown (Jacqueline) 475.00
    12" vinyl, #1338, 1984–1986, Portraits of History (Nancy Drew) 75.00
LADY IN RED — 20", #1134, 1958 only, red taffeta (Cissy) . . . . .1,900.00 up
    10", 1990, Portrette (Cissette) 90.00
LADY IN WAITING — 8" h.p., #487, 1955 only (Wendy Ann) . . . . .1,600.00 up
LADY LEE — 8", #442, 1988 only, Storybook Series 70.00
LADY LOVELACE — Cloth/felt, 1930s 650.00
LADY VALENTINE — 8" #140503, 1994 only (Wendy Ann) 65.00
LADY WINDERMERE — 21" compo., 1945–1946, extra makeup, Portrait Series . . . . .2,500.00 up
LANCELOT — 8", #79529, 1995, 100th Anniversary (copy of 1995 Disney auction doll) 100.00
    8", #13550, 1999, blue and black outfit with sword 80.00
LANE, HARRIET — 1982–1984, 3rd set Presidents' Ladies/First Ladies Series (Mary Ann) 125.00
LAOS — 8" straight leg, #525, 1987–1988 . . . . .70.00
LAPLAND — 8" h.p., #537, 1993 . . . . .70.00
LASSIE — 8", #11102, 1995 only, International Folk Tales (Norway) 65.00
LATVIA — 8" straight leg, #527, 1987 only 75.00
LAUGHING ALLEGRA — Cloth, 1932 . . . . .650.00
LAURA INGALLS WILDER — 8", #14110, 1998–1999,
    patchwork print outfit 75.00
LAURIE, LITTLE MEN — 8" h.p., BK, #781, #755,
    1966–1972 (Wendy Ann) 175.00
    Straight leg, #0755, #416, 1973–1975,
    marked "Alex" 100.00
    Check pants, marked "Alexander" 85.00
    Straight leg, #416, #410, 1976–1992 . . . . .75.00
    8", #14620, 1996, waistcoat, houndstooth trousers . . .65.00
    12" all h.p., 1966 only (Lissy) 625.00
    12" plastic/vinyl, 1967–1988 (Nancy Drew) 75.00
LAURIE, PIPER — 14" h.p., 1950 only (Margaret) . . .2,400.00 up
    21" h.p., 1950 only (Margaret) . . . . .2,900.00 up
LAZY MARY — 7" compo., 1936–1938 (Tiny Betty) 275.00
LEMONADE GIRL — 8", #14130, 1998–1999 (Maggie),
    doll with stand, etc 90.00
LENA (RIVERBOAT QUEEN) —
    (see M.A.D.C. under Special Events/Exclusives)
LENNOX, MARY, — 14" Classic Series, 1993–1994 . . . . . . .100.00
LEO — 8", #21370, 1998, golden lion costume 90.00
LEOPARD WITH SHOPPING BAG — 10", Cissette, 1997–1998 . .125.00
LE PETIT BOUDOIR — 1993
    (see Collectors United under Special Events/Exclusives)
LESLIE (BLACK POLLY) — 17" vinyl, 1965–1971, in dress . .275.00
    1966–1971, as bride 300.00
    1965–1971, in formal or ballgown 375.00

Leslie, 17", #1665, 1970, plastic/vinyl. Tulle dress with lace trim.

Dating Lissy Dolls

12" Lissy and Lissy face dolls are all hard plastic with glued-on wigs.
Lissy is not marked anywhere on the body. Only the clothes were tagged.

1956 – 1958	Lissy had jointed elbows and knees which allow her to sit. Her feet are slightly arched to wear sandals with hose or white socks. The 1957-1958 Lissy Little Women wear black sandals.
1959 – 1967	The Lissy face dolls have the Lissy face but have non-jointed arms and legs. The feet are flat.
1959 – 1967	Lissy face Little Women were made.
1959	Kelly (Lissy face) was produced 1959 only in a variety of outfits.
1962	Pamela (Lissy face) had three interchangeable outfits with extra clothing in a gift set. Pamela has a Velcro strip to attach the wigs. Pamela was made for several years as store specials. Pamela was also made with the later Nancy Drew vinyl head.
1962	Lissy face Katie and Tommy made for FAO Schwarz's 100th Anniversary.
1963	McGuffey Ana, Southern Belle, and Scarlett O'Hara were made using the Lissy face doll.
1965	Brigitta of the large set of Sound of Music was made using the Lissy face doll in an alpine outfit and the rare sailor costume.
1966	Lissy face Cinderellas was available in "poor" outfit or in blue satin ball gown. A gift set featured the doll and both outfits.
1967	Only year Laurie of Little Women was made using the Lissy face.
1993	Nine Lissy face dolls were made for the regular line: Amy, Beth, Jo, Meg, Ballerina, Greta Brinker, Hans Brinker, Hamlet, and Ophelia.
1993	Special for Horchow. Pamela Plays Dress Up was a Lissy face doll with wigs, clothes, and a trunk. Lissy face Alice in Wonderland with Jabberwocky was made for Disney, and the Columbian Sailor was made for the UFDC Luncheon.

LESLIE (BLACK POLLY), CONTINUED...

In trunk with wardrobe . . . . .650.00 up
1966–1971, as ballerina 375.00
LETTY BRIDESMAID — 7–8" compo., 1938–1940 (Tiny Betty) 275.00
LEWIS, SHARI — 14", 1958–1959 . . . . .650.00
21", 1958–1959 . . . . .850.00
LIBERACE WITH CANDELABRA — 8", #22080, 1997, velvet cape 115.00
LIBRA — 8", #21390, 1998, balanced scale headpiece, purple costume 90.00
LIESL — (see Sound of Music)
'LIL CHRISTMAS CANDY — 8" h.p.,#100348, 1994 only, Americana Series 70.00
'LIL CHRISTMAS COOKIE — 8", #341, 1993–1994, Americana Series 70.00
'LIL CLARA AND THE NUTCRACKER — 8", #140480, 1994, Storyland Series 70.00
'LIL SIR GENIUS — 7", #701 & #400701 vinyl, painted eyes, 1993, in blue jumpsuit 50.00
LILA BRIDESMAID — 7–8" compo., 1938–1940 (Tiny Betty) 325.00
LILAC FAIRIE — 21", 1993, Portrait ballerina 300.00
LILIBET — 16" compo., 1938 (Princess Elizabeth) . . . . .750.00 up
LILY — 10", #1114, 1987–1988, red/black (Cissette) 85.00
LILY OF THE VALLEY — 10", satin gown with lilies of the valley 130.00
LINCOLN, MARY TODD — 1982–1984, 3rd set Presidents' Ladies/First Ladies Series (Louisa) 150.00
LIND, JENNY — 21" h.p./vinyl arms, #2191, 1969, dressed in all pink, no trim (Jacqueline) 1,400.00
#2181, 1970, all pink with lace trim 1,500.00
10", #1171, 1969, Portrette, all pink, no trim (Cissette) 600.00
10", #1184, 1970, Portrette, pink with lace trim (Cissette) 650.00
14" plastic/vinyl, #1491, 1970 only, Portrait Children Series (Mary Ann) pink, lace trim 375.00

LIND, JENNY & LISTENING CAT — 14", #1470, 1969–1971, Portrait Children Series,
blue dot dress apron & holds plush kitten (must have kitten) (Mary Ann) .325.00
LION TAMER — 8", #306, 1990, Americana Series (Wendy Ann) 70.00
LISSY — 11½"–12" h.p., 1956–1958, jointed knees & elbows
    1956–1958, as ballerina 425.00
    1956–1958, as bride . . . . .425.00 up
    1956–1957, as bridesmaid . . . . .650.00 up
    1958, dressed in formal . . . . .500.00 up
    1956–1958, in street dresses . . . . .350.00 up
    1956, in window box with wardrobe . . . . .1,500.00 up
    21", one-piece arm, pink tulle pleated skirt (Cissy) 1,300.00
    21", #2051, 1966, pink with tiara (Coco) 2,200.00
    12" h.p., 1957, jointed elbows & knees, in window box with wardrobe (Lissy) . . . . . .1,400.00 up
    12" h.p., one-piece arms & legs in window box/wardrobe, 1959–1966 (Lissy) . . . . .1,000.00 up
    Classics (see individuals, example: McGuffey Ana, Scarlett, Cinderella)
LITHUANIA — 8" h.p., #110544, 1994 only (Maggie) 65.00
LITTLE ANGEL — 9" latex/vinyl, 1950–1957 . . . . .200.00
LITTLE AUDREY — Vinyl, 1954 only . . . . .475.00 up
LITTLE BETTY — 9–11" compo., 1935–1943, must be mint 250.00–325.00
LITTLE BITSEY — 9" all vinyl nurser, 1967–1968 (Sweet Tears) 150.00
LITTLE BO PEEP — (see Bo Peep, Little)
LITTLE BOY BLUE — 7" compo., 1937–1939 (Tiny Betty) 300.00
LITTLE BUTCH — 9" all vinyl nurser, 1967–1968 (Sweet Tears) .150.00
LITTLE CHERUB — 11" compo., 1945–1946 . . . . .275.00
    7" all vinyl, 1960 only 250.00
LITTLE CHRISTMAS PRINCESS — 8", #10369, 1996 Holiday 65.00
LITTLE COLONEL — 8½–9" compo. (*rare size*),
    1935, closed mouth (Betty) 650.00
    11–13" compo. (*rare size*),
      closed mouth (Betty) 550.00–650.00
    17" compo., closed mouth (Betty) . . . . .750.00 up
    14", open mouth (Betty) 650.00
    17"–23", open mouth 750.00–950.00
    26–27", open mouth . . . . .1,250.00 up
LITTLE DEVIL — 8" h.p., Americana Series,
    1992–1993 only 85.00
LITTLE DORRIT — 16" cloth, early 1930s,
    Dickens character 700.00
LITTLE EDWARDIAN — 8" h.p., SL, SLW, #0200, 1953–1955,
    long dotted navy gown . . . . .950.00 up
LITTLE EMILY — 16" cloth, early 1930s,
    Dickens character 650.00
LITTLE EMPEROR — 8" (see U.F.D.C. under Special Events/Exclusives)
LITTLE GENIUS — 12–14" compo./cloth, 1935–1940,
    1942–1946 . . . . .200.00
    16–20" compo./cloth, 1935–1937, 1942–1946 . . . . .250.00
    24–25", 1936–1940 . . . . .250.00
    8" h.p./vinyl, 1956–1962, nude (clean condition),
      good face color .100.00
      Dressed in cotton play dress 175.00
      In dressy, lacy outfit with bonnet 275.00
      Dressed in christening outfit 350.00
      Sewing or Gift Set, 1950s . . . . .850.00 up
    7" vinyl, 1993–1995, reintroduced doll
      with painted eyes 50.00

Lissy, 12", 1956, with black eyes with no pupils. All original and tagged "Lissy."

L

#701 & 400701, 1993–1995, dressed in blue jumpsuit (Lil' Sir Genius) .50.00
#702 & 400702, 1993–1995, dressed in pink lacy dress (Lil' Miss Genius) 55.00
1993, extra packaged outfits . . . . .30.00 each
Christening Baby, #400703, 1994-1995 . . . . .50.00
Super Genius, #400704, 1994–1995, dressed in Superman style outfit 50.00
Birthday Party, #400705, 1994 only 50.00
Genius Elf, #400706, 1994–1995, dressed in Christmas red and green 50.00

LITTLE GODEY — 8" h.p., #491, 1953–1955 (Wendy Ann) . . . . .1,100.00 up
LITTLE GRANNY — 14" plastic/vinyl, #1431, 1966 only, floral gown (Mary Ann) 250.00
   14", #1430, 1966 only, pinstriped gown (also variations) (Mary Ann) 225.00
LITTLE HUGGUMS — (see Huggums)
LITTLE JACK HORNER — 7" compo., 1937–1943 (Tiny Betty) 300.00
LITTLE JUMPING JOAN — 8", #487, 1989–1990, Storybook Series (Maggie Mixup) 75.00
LITTLE LADY DOLL — 8" h.p., #1050, 1960 only, gift set in mint condition (Maggie Mixup) . . . . . . .800.00 up
   8" doll only, must have correct hairdo and excellent face color 350.00
   21" h.p., 1949, has braids & colonial gown, extra makeup, Portrait Series (Wendy Ann) 2,400.00
LITTLE LORD FAUNTLEROY — Cloth, 1930s 750.00
   13" compo., 1936–1937 (Wendy Ann) . . . . .650.00 up
LITTLE MADELINE — 8" h.p., 1953–1954 (Wendy Ann) . . . . .750.00 up
LITTLE MAID — 8" straight leg, #423, 1987–1988, Storybook Series (Wendy Ann) 70.00
LITTLE MEN — 15" h.p., 1950–1952 (Margaret & Maggie) . . . . .850.00 each
LITTLE MEN — Set with Tommy, Nat & Stuffy, must be in excellent condition . . . . .2,600.00 set
LITTLE MERMAID — 10", #1145, 1992–1993, Portrette, green/blue outfit (Cissette) 115.00
   8", #14531, 1995, Hans Christian Andersen Series, has long black hair 65.00
LITTLE MINISTER — 8" h.p., #411, 1957 only (Wendy Ann) . . . . .3,000.00 up
LITTLE MISS — 8" h.p., #489, 1989–1991 only, Storybook Series (Maggie Mixup) 75.00
LITTLE MISS GODEY — (see M.A.D.C. under Special Events/Exclusives)
LITTLE MISS MAGNIN — (see I. Magnin under Special Events/Exclusives)
LITTLE NANNIE ETTICOAT — #428, 1986–1988, straight leg, Storybook Series 85.00
LITTLE NELL — 16" cloth, early 1930s, Dickens character . . . . .650.00 up
   14" compo., 1938–1940 (Wendy Ann) 675.00
LITTLE ORPHAN ANNIE — 8", #13740, 1999, red dress, comes with dog Sandy 50.00
LITTLE PRINCESS — 14", #26415, 1995 only, has trunk and wardrobe (Louisa) 250.00
LITTLE PRINCESS, A — 8", #14120, 1998–1999, pink taffeta, with doll 90.00
LITTLE SHAVER — 10" cloth, 1940–1944 . . . . .450.00 up
   7" cloth, 1940–1944 . . . . .550.00
   15" cloth, 1940–1944 . . . . .600.00
   22" cloth, 1940–1944 . . . . .650.00 up
   12" cloth, 1941–1943 (see Baby Shaver)
   12" plastic/vinyl, 1963–1965, has painted eyes 250.00
LITTLE SOUTHERN BOY/GIRL — 10" latex/vinyl, 1950–1951 . . . . .150.00 each
LITTLE SOUTHERN GIRL — 8" h.p., #305, 1953 only (Wendy Ann) .950.00 up

Little Minister (center), 8", #411, 1957 only, with 1953 Quizkin Bride and Groom.

LITTLE THUMBKINS — 8", #14532, Hans Christian Andersen Series, lavender/pink/yellow tiers 65.00
LITTLE VICTORIA — 7½"–8", #376, 1953–1954 only (Wendy Ann) . . . . .1,200.00 up
LITTLE WOMEN — Meg, Jo, Amy, Beth (Marme in sets when available)

    16" cloth, 1930–1936 . . . . .700.00 up each

    7" compo., 1935–1944 (Tiny Betty) . . . . .325.00 each

    9" compo., 1937–1940 (Little Betty) . . . . .300.00 each

    13–15" compo., 1937–1946 (Wendy Ann) . . . . .350.00 each

    14–15" h.p., 1947–1956, plus Marme (Margaret & Maggie) . . . . 450.00 each . . . .2,200.00 set

    14"–15" h.p., widespread fingers, ca. 1949–1952 . . . . .475.00 each

    14–15" h.p., BK, plus Marme (Margaret & Maggie) . . . . 450.00 each . . . .2,200.00 set

    14–15" Amy with loop curls, must have good face color (Margaret) . . . . .550.00 each

    8" Amy with loop curls, 1991 #411 . . . . .95.00 each

    7½–8" h.p., SL, SLW, all #609, 1955, plus Marme (Wendy Ann) . . . . .375.00 each . . .1,800.00 set

    8" h.p., BKW, all #609, all #409, all #481, 1956–1959 (Wendy Ann) . . . . . . .300.00 each . . .1,500.00 set

    8" BKW, all #381, 1960–1963 (Wendy Ann) . . . . 250.00 each . . .1,200.00 set

        #781, 1964–1972 . . . . 125.00 each . . . . .650.00 set

        #7811 to #7815, 1973 . . . . 100.00 each . . . . .550.00 set

    8" straight leg, #411 to #415, 1974–1986 . . . . 75.00 each . . . . .375.00 set

        #405 to #409, 1987–1990 . . . . 65.00 each . . . . .350.00 set

        #411 to #415, 1991–1992 . . . . 65.00 each . . . . .350.00 set

        #14523–14528, 1995 . . . . .60.00 each . . . . .300.00 set

        Exclusive for FAO Schwarz (see Special Events/Exclusives)

    10", #14630–14633, 1996 . . . . .85.00 each . . . . .375.00 set

    11½–12" h.p., jointed elbows & knees, 1957–1958 (Lissy) . . . . 375.00 each . . .1,900.00 set

    11½–12" h.p., one-piece arms & legs, 1959–1968 (Lissy) . . . . .300.00 each . . .1,500.00 set

    12" plastic/vinyl, 1969–1982 (Nancy Drew) . . . . 65.00 each . . . . .325.00 set

    12" plastic/vinyl, 1983–1989, new outfits (Nancy Drew) . . . . 65.00 each . . . . .325.00 set

    12", 1989–1990 only (see Sears unders Special Events/Exclusives)

    12", 1993 only, no Marme (Lissy) . . . . 100.00 each

    16", 1997–1999, plastic/vinyl, Little Women Journal Series (no Marme) . . . . . .105.00 each

    16", 1999, Marmee, #28040, Little Women Journals 125.00

Meg, 8", 1955, Little
Women, hard plastic
(Wendy).

Meg, 15", #1500, 1952,
Little Women, hard
plastic (Margaret).

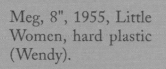

Little Women Beth,
15", 1949 (Maggie),
hard plastic. Dress
tagged: "Beth."

LITTLEST KITTEN — 8" vinyl, 1963, nude, clean, good face color . . . . .125.00 up
    Dressed in lacy dress oufit with bonnet . . . . .275.00 up
    Dressed in christening outfit . . . . .325.00 up
    In sewing or gift set . . . . .700.00 up
    Dressed in play attire 175.00
LIVELY HUGGUMS — 25", knob makes limbs and head move, 1963 . . . . .150.00
LIVELY KITTEN — 14", 18", 24", 1962–1963, knob makes limbs and head move 100.00–175.00
LIVELY PUSSY CAT — 14", 20", 24", 1966–1969, knob makes limbs and head move 100.00–175.00
LOLA AND LOLLIE BRIDESMAID — 7" compo., 1938–1940 (Tiny Betty) . . . . 300.00 up each
LOLLIE BABY — Rubber/compo, 1941–1942 . . . . .100.00
LOLLIPOP MUNCHKIN — (see Munchkin)
LOOBY LOO — 15½" h.p., ca. 1951–1954 . . . . .675.00 up
LORD FAUNTLEROY — 12", 1981–1983, Portrait Children (Nancy Drew) 95.00
LORD VALENTINE — 8" #140502, 1994 only (Wendy Ann) 75.00
LOUISA — (see Sound of Music)
LOVE — 8" (see Collectors United under Specials Events/Exclusives)
    8", made for public in 1994 (Only differences on C.U. doll are gold locket, pearls set into cap, and
       gold metal braids on slippers, heart box) 75.00
LOVEY DOVE (DOVEY) — 19" vinyl baby, 1958–1959, closed mouth, molded or rooted hair, few are mistagged .175.00
    19" h.p./latex, 1950–1951 . . . . .125.00
    12" all h.p. toddler, 1948–1951 (Precious) . . . . .375.00 up
       1951, dressed as "Ringbearer" . . . . .650.00 up
    "Answer Doll" with lever in back to move head . . . . .525.00 up
LUCINDA — 12" plastic/vinyl, 1969–1970 (Janie) . . . . .350.00 up
    14" plastic/vinyl, #1435, #1535, 1971–1982 (11 year production), blue gown (Mary Ann) 100.00
    14", #1535, 1983–1986, Classic Series, pink or peach gown (Mary Ann) .90.00
LUCK OF THE IRISH — 8", #327, 1992–1993 only, Americana Series (Maggie Mixup) 70.00
LUCY — 8" h.p., #488, 1961 only, Americana Series, strip cotton/poke bonnet (Wendy Ann) . . . . . .1,800.00 up
LUCY BRIDE — 14" h.p., 1949–1950 (Margaret) . . . . .900.00 up
    18" h.p., 1949–1950 (Margaret) . . . . .900.00 up
    21" h.p., 1949–1950 (Margaret) 1,100.00
    21", #2155, 1955, (Cissy) pale pink gown, very red hair, heavily painted face . . . . .5,000.00 up
    14" compo., 1937–1940 (Wendy Ann) 450.00
    17" compo., 1937–1940 (Wendy Ann) 550.00

Madelaine Du Bain, composition, 1937–1941. All original with wrist tag.

    21" compo., 1942–1944, Portrait,
       extra make-up (Wendy Ann) . . .2,500.00
LUCY LOCKET — 8" straight leg, #433, 1986–1988,
    Storybook Series 85.00
    14", #25501, 1995, Ribbons & Bows Series,
       purple floral skirt (Louisa) 150.00
LUCY RICARDO — (see FAO Schwarz under
    Special Events/Exclusives) 150.00
    9", '50s gingham dress,
       with bottle and spoon 115.00
    21", #50003, 1996 Timeless Legends,
       black dress with black and white polka
       dots accents 325.00
    10", #14071, Shadow Polka Dot Lucy,
       1998–1999 . . . . .175.00
    10", #15160, 1999, Lucy's Italian Movie,
       peasant outfit, grape vat 160.00
LUCY AND RICKY — 9" set, Vitameatavegamin
    episode 200.00
LULLABY MUNCHKIN — (see Munchkin)

PLEASE READ "WHAT IS A PRICE GUIDE?" FOR ADDITIONAL INFORMATION

MAD HATTER — 8", #14510, 1995, Alice in Wonderland Series 75.00
M.A.D.C. (MADAME ALEXANDER DOLL CLUB) — (see Special Events/Exclusives)
MADAME BUTTERFLY — 10" (see Marshall Fields under Special Events/Exclusives)
    8", h.p., #22000, 1997 – 1998, shadow, kimono 95.00
    21", #22010, 1997, kimono over silk robe 350.00
MADAME DOLL — 21" h.p./vinyl arms, 1966 only, pink brocade (Coco) ....2,200.00 up
    14" plastic/vinyl, #1460, #1561, 1967–1975, Classic Series (Mary Ann) 275.00
MADAME (ALEXANDER) — 21", 1984 only, one-piece skirt in pink 400.00
    21", 1985–1987, pink with overskirt that unsnaps 275.00
    21", 1988–1990, blue with full lace overskirt 275.00
    21", #79507, 1995, 100th Anniversary, pink with lace jacket, limited edition of 500 ....750.00
    8", 1993 only, introduced mid-year (see Madame Alexander Doll Co. under Special Events/Exclusives)
    8" in blue gown (see Doll & Teddy Bear Expo. under Special Events/Exclusives)
    8", #79527, 1995, 100th Anniversary 100.00
MADAME ALEXANDER COLLECTOR'S PHONOGRAPH ALBUM —1978, Madame's voice reading children's stories ..35.00
MADAME POMPADOUR — 21" h.p./vinyl arms, #2197, 1970, pink lace overskirt (Jacqueline) 1,200.00
MADELAINE — 14" compo., 1940–1942 (Wendy Ann) 625.00
    8" h.p., 1954, FAO Schwarz special ....800.00 up
MADELAINE DU BAIN — 11" compo., closed mouth, 1937 (Wendy Ann) 500.00
    14" compo., 1938–1939 (Wendy Ann) ....550.00 up
    17" compo., 1939–1941 (Wendy Ann) ....675.00 up
    21" compo., 1939–1941 (Wendy Ann) ....900.00 up
    14" h.p., 1949–1951 (Maggie) ....950.00 up
MADELINE — 17–18" h.p./jointed elbows & knees, 1950–1953 ....800.00 up
    18" h.p., 1961 only, vinyl head, extra jointed body, wears short dress, must be mint ....700.00 up
      Ballgown 1961 only ....800.00 up

Maggie Mixup, 8", 1960 – 1961, h.p. (Maggie), original outfit. Tagged: "Maggie". Red felt flowers on blue striped pants.

MADISON, DOLLY — 1976–1978, 1st set Presidents' Ladies/First Ladies Series (Martha) 125.00
MADONNA AND CHILD — 10", #10600, 1995, Christmas Series 105.00
MAGGIE — 15" h.p., 1948–1954 (Little Women only to 1956) 550.00
    17–18", 1949–1953 ....650.00 up
    20–21", 1948–1954 ....700.00 up
    22–23", 1949–1952 ....800.00 up
    17" plastic/vinyl, 1972–1973 only (Elise) 175.00
MAGGIE ELF — 8", #14585, 1995, Christmas Series 70.00
MAGGIE MIXUP — 16½" h.p./vinyl, 1960 only (Elise body) 375.00
    17" plastic/vinyl, 1961 only ....400.00 up
    8" h.p., #600, #611, #617, #627, 1960–1961, freckles ....450.00 up
    8" Wendy Ann face, freckles 450.00
    8" h.p., #618, 1961, as angel 750.00
    8", #610, 1960–1961, dressed in overalls and has watering can 750.00
    8", #626, 1960–1961, dressed in skater outfit ...700.00 up
    8", #634, 1960–1961, dressed in riding habit 550.00
    8", #593, 1960, dressed in roller skating outfit 750.00
    8", #598, #597, #596, 1960, wearing dresses or skirts/blouses ....425.00 up
    8", #31000, 1997 – 1998, Post Office commemorative, blue gingham 75.00

MAGGIE TEENAGER — 15–18" h.p., 1951–1953 . . . . .475.00–600.00 up
   23", 1951–1953 . . . . .650.00 up
MAGGIE WALKER — 15–18" h.p., 1949–1953 . . . . .400.00–575.00
   20–21", 1949–1953 . . . . .575.00
   23–25", 1951–1953 (with Cissy face) . . . . .650.00 up
MAGNOLIA — 21", #2297, 1977 only, many rows of lace on pink gown 500.00
   21", #2251, 1988 only, yellow gown 300.00
MAID MARIAN — 8" h.p., #492, 1989–1991 only, Storybook Series (Wendy Ann) 125.00
   21", 1992–1993 only, Portrait Series (Jacqueline) 325.00
MAID OF HONOR — 18" compo., 1940–1944 (Wendy Ann) . . . . .700.00 up
   14" plastic/vinyl, #1592, 1988–1989, Classic Series, blue gown (Mary Ann) 100.00
MAJORETTE — 14–17" compo., 1937–1938 (Wendy Ann) . . . . .850.00 up
DRUM MAJORETTE — 8" h.p., #482, 1955 only (Wendy Ann) . . . . .950.00 up
   8", #314, 1991–1992 only, Americana Series, no baton 70.00
MALI — 8", #11565, 1996 International, African-American print costume 65.00
MAMBO — 8", h.p., #481, 1955 only (Wendy Ann) . . . . .700.00 up
MAMMY — 8", #402, 1989 only, Jubilee II set (black "round" face) 100.00
   8" h.p., #635, 1991–1992 only, Scarlett Series (black Wendy Ann on Cissette body) 100.00
   10" h.p., #15010, 1997–1999 (black Wendy Ann) 95.00
MANET — 21", #2225, 1982–1983, light brown with dark brown pinstripes (Jacqueline) 250.00
   14", #1571, 1986–1987, Fine Arts Series (Mary Ann) 85.00
MARCELLA DOLLS — 13–24" compo., 1936 only, dressed in 1930s fashions . . . . .650.00–900.00 each
MARCH HARE — Cloth/felt, mid 1930s 675.00
MARGARET (O'BRIEN) — 14" h.p., nude with excellent color . . . . . .275.00   18" . . . . . .550.00 up
   14" h.p. in tagged Alexander boxed clothes . . . . .475.00   18" . . . . .650.00 up
   21" compo., tagged Alexander clothes . . . . .1,250.00 up
MARGARET ANN — 15", #90100, 1999, blue dress, straw hat, porcelain 140.00
MARGARET ROSE — (see Princess Margaret Rose)
MARGOT — 10–11" h.p., 1961 only, in formals (Cissette) . . . . .475.00 up
   Street dresses, bathing suit, 1961 only 350.00
MARGOT BALLERINA — 15–18", 1951–1953, dressed in various colored outfits
   (Margaret & Maggie) 675.00–750.00
   15–18" h.p./vinyl arms, 1955 only (Cissy) 375.00–475.00

Margot, 10", 1961, hard plastic (Cissette). Mint, tagged outfit.

Margot Ballerina, 1951, all hard plastic (Maggie). All original.

MARIA — (see Sound of Music)
MARIE ANTOINETTE — 21", #2248, 1987–1988, multi-floral
    print with pink front insert (Jacqueline) 425.00
    21" compo., 1944–1946, Portrait with extra makeup
    and in mint condition (Wendy Ann) 2,100.00
MARILLA — 10", #261-168, 1994,
    Anne of Green Gables Series 95.00
MARINE — 14" compo., 1943–1944 (Wendy Ann as boy) ...800.00
MARIONETTES/TONY SARG — 12–14" compo., 1934–1940 ...475.00 up
    12" compo., Disney Characters ....475.00 up
MARLEY'S GHOST — 8", #18004, 1996, Dickens,
    silver chains 65.00
MARM LIZA — 21" compo., 1938 and 1946, extra makeup,
    mint condition (Wendy Ann) ....3,200.00 up
MARME — (see Little Women)
MARSHALL FIELDS — (see Special Events/Exclusives)
MARTA — (see Sound of Music)
MARTIN, MARY — 14–17" h.p., 1948–1952,
    wearing jumpsuit (Margaret) 700.00–875.00
    14–17", 1948–1952, dressed in sailor suit or ballgown
    (Nell from *South Pacific*) 800.00–975.00
MARY, JOSEPH, BABY JESUS IN MANGER — 8", #19470,
    1997–1999, Nativity set 190.00
MARY ANN — 14" plastic/vinyl, 1965, tagged "Mary Ann",
    in red/white dress 250.00
    Dressed in skirt and sweater 250.00
    Ballerina 250.00
    14" ballerina, 1973–1982 ....125.00

Maid of Honor, 14", #1592, plastic/vinyl (Mary Ann). Made from 1988 – 1989. Classic Series.

    14", reintroduced #241599, 1994 only 75.00
MARYBEL "THE DOLL THAT GETS WELL" — 16" rigid vinyl, 1959–1965, doll only 200.00
    1959, 1961, 1965, doll in case 350.00
    1960 only, doll in case with wardrobe 400.00
    1965 only, doll with very long straight hair, in case 425.00
    75th Anniversary Marybel Returns, 1998, #12220 ....155.00
MARY CASSATT BABY — 14" cloth/vinyl, 1969–1970 ....175.00
    20", 1969–1970 ....250.00
    14" plastic/vinyl child, #1566, 1987 only, Fine Arts Series (Mary Ann) 90.00
MARY ELLEN — 31" rigid vinyl, walker, 1954 only ....600.00 up
    31" plastic/vinyl arms, 1955 only, non-walker with jointed elbows ....500.00 up
MARY ELLEN PLAYMATE — 16" plastic/vinyl, 1965 only, Marshall Fields exclusive (Mary Ann) 325.00
    12", 1965, in case with wigs (Lissy) ....850.00 up
    17", 1965, exclusive 350.00
MARY GRAY — 14" plastic/vinyl, #1564, 1988 only, Classic Series (Mary Ann) 85.00
MARY HAD A LITTLE LAMB — 8", #14623, 1996 Nursery Rhyme, #11610, 1997–1999 ....75.00
MARY LENNOX — 14", #1537, 1993–1994, Classic Doll Series 95.00
    8", h.p., #13850, 1998–1999 (Secret Garden), plaid jumper, holds key 80.00
MARY LOUISE — 21" compo., 1938, 1946–1947, golden brown/burnt orange (Wendy Ann) 2,700.00
    18" h.p., 1954 only, Me & My Shadow Series, burnt orange & olive green (Cissy) ....1,300.00 up
    8" h.p., #0035D, 1954 only, same as 18", Me & My Shadow Series (Wendy Ann) ....1,200.00 up
MARY, MARY — 8" h.p., BKW, BK, #751, 1965–1972, Storybook Series (Wendy Ann) 125.00
    8" h.p., straight leg, #0751, #451, 1973–1975, marked "Alex" 75.00
    8" h.p., straight leg, #451, 1976–1987, marked "Alexander" (1985–1987 white face) 65.00
    8", #471, reintroduced 1992 only (Wendy Ann) 60.00
    8", #14556, 1996, floral dress, straw hat, #11600, 1997–1999, water can 75.00
    14", #1569, 1988–1991, Classic Series (Mary Ann) 80.00
    14", #241595, reintroduced 1994 only 100.00
MARY MINE — 21" cloth/vinyl, 1977–1989 ....125.00
    14" cloth/vinyl, 1977–1979 ....100.00
    14", reintroduced 1989 ....75.00
MARY MUSLIN — 19" cloth, 1951 only, pansy eyes 500.00

M

26", 1951 only 575.00
40", 1951 only 850.00
MARY, QUEEN OF SCOTS — 21", #2252, 1988–1989 (Jacqueline) 375.00
MARY ROSE BRIDE — 17" h.p., 1951 only (Margaret) . . . . .750.00 up
MARY SUNSHINE, LITTLE — 15" plastic/vinyl, 1961 (Caroline) .375.00
MARZIPAN DANCER — 10", #14573, 1995, Nutcracker Series (Cissette) 75.00
MATTHEW — 8", #26424, 1995, Anne of Green Gables Series 65.00
McELROY, MARY — 1985–1987, 4th set Presidents' Ladies/First Ladies Series (Mary Ann) 125.00
McGUFFEY ANA — 16" cloth, 1934–1936 . . . . .675.00
    7" compo., 1935–1939 (Tiny Betty) 350.00
    9" compo., 1935–1939 (Little Betty) 375.00
    15" compo., 1935–1937 (Betty) 650.00
    13" compo., 1938 (Wendy Ann) 650.00
    11", 1937–1939, has closed mouth 675.00
    11–13" compo., 1937–1944 (Princess Elizabeth) 675.00
    14–16" compo., 1937–1944 (Princess Elizabeth) 675.00
    17–20" compo., 1937–1943 (Princess Elizabeth) .700.00–1,200.00
    21–25" compo., 1937–1942 (Princess Elizabeth) .750.00–1,400.00
    28" compo., 1937–1939 (Princess Elizabeth) 1,400.00
    17" compo., 1948–1949 (Margaret) 900.00
    14½" compo., 1948, wears coat, hat & muff 950.00
    18", 25", 31", 1955–1956, has flat feet (Cissy) 500.00–950.00
    18" h.p., 1949–1950 (Margaret) 900.00
    21" h.p., 1948–1950 (Margaret) 1,400.00
    12" h.p. (*rare doll),* 1963 only (Lissy) . . . . .2,000.00 up
    8" h.p., #616, 1956 only (Wendy Ann) 750.00
    8" h.p., #788, #388, 1963–1965 (was "American Girl" in 1962–1963) 350.00
    8", #496, 1990–1991 only, Storybook Series (Wendy Ann) 80.00
    29" cloth/vinyl, 1952 only (Barbara Jane) 650.00
    15", porcelain, #90110 . . . . .165.00
McGUFFEY ANA
    14" plastic/vinyl, #1450, 1968–1969, Classic Series, wears plaid dress/eyelet apron (Mary Ann) 120.00
    14" plastic/vinyl, #1525, 1977–1986, Classic Series, wears plaid dress (Mary Ann) 85.00
    14" plastic/vinyl, #1526, 1987–1988, mauve stripe pinafore, Classic Series (Mary Ann) 85.00

McGuffey Ana, 18", 1949, all hard plastic (Margaret). All original.

Mclanie, 10", #1182, 1970, hard plastic (Cissette), all original.

14", #24622, 1995, red plaid dress,
   Nostalgia Series (Mary Ann) .90.00
McKee, Mary — 1985–1987, 4th set Presidents' Ladies/First
   Ladies Series (Mary Ann) 125.00
McKinley, Ida — 1988, 5th set Presidents' Ladies/First
   Ladies Series (Louisa) 125.00
Me and My Scassi — (see FAO Schwarz under Special Events/Exclusives)
Meagan — 14", #29990 or #30000, 1999 . . . . .80.00
Medici, Catherine de — 21" porcelain, 1990–1991 . . . . .500.00
Meg — 8", #79530, 100th Anniversary, two-tiered blue gown
   with white and rose trim (also see Little Women) 100.00
Melanie — 21" compo., 1945–1947 (Wendy Ann) . . . . .2,300.00 up
   21" h.p./vinyl arms, 1961,
     lace bodice & overdress over satin (Cissy) . . . . .975.00 up
   21", #2050, 1966, blue gown with wide lace
     down sides (Coco) . . . . .2,200.00 up
   #2173, 1967, blue dress with white rick-rack around
     hem ruffle (Jacqueline) .625.00
   #2181, 1968, rust brown dress and hat 500.00
   #2193, 1969, blue gown, white trim,
     many rows of lace, bonnet 525.00
   #2196, 1970, white gown with red ribbon trim 525.00
   #2162, 1971, blue gown, white sequin trim 450.00
   #2195, 1974, white gown, red jacket and bonnet 475.00
   #2220, 1979–1980, white dotted swiss gown with pink trim 325.00
   1981, pink nylon with blue ribbon 325.00
   #2254, 1989, all orange with lace shawl 300.00
   10", #1173, 1968–1969, pink multi-tiered skirt (Cissette) 450.00
   10", #1182, 1970, yellow multi-tiered skirt 475.00
   8" h.p., #633, 1955–1956, green velvet (Wendy Ann) . . . . .1,100.00 up
   12", 1987 only, Portrait Children Series, aqua green gown, brown trim (Nancy Drew) 80.00
   10", #1101, 1989 only, Jubilee II, all royal blue dress with black trim (Cissette) 125.00
   8", #627, 1990, Scarlett Series,
     lavender/lace (Wendy Ann) 100.00
   8", #628, 1992, peach gown/bonnet with lace 95.00
   10", #16555, 1996, Melanie's Sewing Circle, blue dress 95.00
Melinda — 10" h.p., 1968–1969, blue gown with white trim (Cissette) 450.00
   10" h.p., 1970, yellow multi-tiered lace skirt 425.00
   22", #1912, 1962 only, wears white organdy dress with red trim 375.00
   14", 16", 22" plastic/vinyl, 1962–1963, cotton dress . . . . .275.00–375.00 up
   14", 16", 22" plastic/vinyl, 1963, party dress 350.00–475.00
   14", 1963 only, as ballerina 350.00
Melody and Friend — 25" and 8"
   (see Madame Alexander Doll Co. under Special Events/Exclusives)
Merlin — 8", #13560, 1999, red velvet robe and crystal ball 80.00
Merry Angel — 8" (see Spiegel's under Special Events/Exclusives)
Metroplex Doll Club — (see Special Events/Exclusives)
Mexico — 7" compo., 1936 (Tiny Betty) 275.00
   9" compo., 1938–1939 (Little Betty) 300.00
   8" h.p., BKW, #776, 1964–1965 (Wendy Ann) .125.00
   8" h.p., BK, #776, 1965–1972 . . . . .100.00
   8" straight leg, #0776, 1973–1975, marked "ALEX" 75.00
   8" straight leg, #576, #550, #520, 1976–1991, marked "Alexander" (1985–1987) 65.00
   8", #11551, 1995 only (Maggie) 60.00
   8", #24100, 1997 – 1998, Mariachi outfit, guitar 75.00
Michael — 11" plastic/vinyl, 1969 only (Janie) (Peter Pan set) with teddy bear 375.00
   8", #468, 1992–1993, Storybook Series (Peter Pan set) (Wendy) 75.00
Midnight — 21", #2256, 1990, dark blue/black (Jacqueline) 300.00

Mary Sunshine, 15", 1961 only.
Fully jointed, plastic/vinyl doll.
Original clothes.

MILLER'S DAUGHTER — 14" with 8" Rumpelstilskin, #1569, 1992 only, limited to 3,000 sets . . . . .300.00 set
MILLY 17" plastic/vinyl, 1968 only (Polly) 375.00
MIMI — 30", h.p. in 1961 only, multi-jointed body, dressed in formal 950.00
    Dressed in romper suit/skirt 550.00
    Dressed in Tyrolean outfit 950.00
    Dressed in slacks, stripe top, straw hat 600.00
    Dressed in red sweater, plaid skirt 600.00
    21" h.p./vinyl arms, #2170, 1971, vivid pink cape & trim on white gown (Jacqueline) 500.00
    14", #1411, 1983–1986, Opera Series (Mary Ann) 90.00
MINISTER, LITTLE — 8" h.p., #411, 1957 only . . . . .3,000.00 up
MIRACLE SANTA — 10", 1996, with street sign 155.00
MIRACLE WENDY — 8", 1996 . . . . .170.00
MISS AMERICA — 14" compo., 1941–1943, holds flag . . . . .850.00 up
MISS ELIZA DOOLITTLE — 10", #20112, 1996 Classic 100.00
MISS GULCH WITH BICYCLE, TOTO — 10", #13240, 1997–1999, Wizard of Oz Series 125.00
MISS LEIGH — 8", 1989, made for C.U. Gathering (see Special Events/Exclusives)
MISS LIBERTY — 10" (see M.A.D.C. under Special Events/Exclusives)
MISS MAGNIN — 10" (see I. Magnin under Special Events/Exclusives)
MISS MUFFETT, LITTLE — 8" h.p., BK, #752, 1965–1972, Storybook Series (Wendy Ann) 125.00
    8" straight leg, #0752, #452, 1973–1975, marked "Alex" 75.00
    8" straight leg, #452, 1976–1986 (1985–1986 white face), marked "Alexander" (Wendy) 65.00
    8" straight leg, #452, 1987–1988 (Maggie) 65.00
    8", #493, 1993, Storybook Series #140493, 1994 . . . . .65.00
    8", #13500, 1998–1999, comes with bowl, spoon, and pillow 90.00
MISS SCARLETT — 14" (see Belk & Leggett under Special Events/Exclusives)
MISS SMARTY — 8", #17610, 1999 (Maggie) pink check outfit 70.00
MISS UNITY — 10" (see U.F.D.C. under Special Events/Exclusives)
MISS U.S.A. — 8" h.p., BK, #728, 1966–1968, Americana Series (Wendy Ann) 325.00
MISS VICTORY — 20" compo., 1944–1946, magnets in hands (Princess Elizabeth) . . . . .750.00 up
MISTERIOSO — 10" h.p., #20119, 1996 Cirque du Soleil Series 85.00
MISTRESS MARY — 7" compo., 1937–1941 (Tiny Betty) 300.00
MOLLY — 14", #1561, 1988 only, Classic Series (Mary Ann) 85.00
MOLLY COTTONTAIL — Cloth/felt, 1930s 625.00
MOMMY & ME — 14" and 7" compo., 1948–1949 (Margaret and Tiny Betty) . . . . .1,700.00 up set
MOMMY & ME ON-THE-GO — 8", 10", h.p., #11010, 1997 – 1998 . . . . .160.00
MOMMY & ME AT HOME — 8", 10", h.p., #11009, 1997 – 1998, pink floral outfits 160.00
MOMMY'S PET — 14–20", 1977–1986 . . . . .50.00–150.00 up
MONA LISA, DAVINCI'S — 8", h.p., 1997, #22140, green velvet dress 80.00
MONET — 21", #2245, 1984–1985, black & white check gown with red jacket (Jacqueline) 275.00
MONIQUE — 8" (see Disney under Specials Events/Exclusives)
MONROE, ELIZABETH — 1976–1978, 1st set Presidents' Ladies/First Ladies Series (Mary Ann) 150.00
MOP-TOP ANNIE — 8", #14486, 1995, red dress with white dots 70.00
MOP-TOP BABY GIRL — 12", #29030, 1998, yarn hair, patchwork dress 55.00
MOP-TOP WENDY — 8" #140484, 1993–1999, Toy Shelf Series 65.00
MOP-TOP BILLY — 8" #140485, 1993–1999, Toy Shelf Series 65.00
MORISOT — 21", #2236, 1985–1986 only, lime green gown with white lace (Jacqueline) 275.00
MORNING GLORY — 14", #25505, Ribbons & Bows Series, floral dress with lace (Mary Ann) 150.00
MOROCCO — 8" h.p., BK, #762, 1968–1970 (Wendy Ann) 275.00
    8", h.p. #11559, 1996 International, belly dancer 65.00
MOSS ROSE — 14", #1559, 1991 only, Classic Series (Louisa) 150.00
MOTHER & ME — 14–15" and 9" compo., 1940–1943, mint condition (Wendy Ann & Little Betty) . . . .1,400.00 up
MOTHER GOOSE — 8" straight leg, #427, #459, 1986–1992, Storybook Series (Wendy Ann) 70.00
    8", #11620, 1997–1999, with goose and book of rhymes 70.00
MOTHER GOTHEL AND RAPUNZEL — 8" & 14", #1539, 1993–1994, limited to 3,000 sets. . . . . .250.00 set
MOTHER HUBBARD — 8", #439, #459, 1988–1989, Storyland Series (Wendy) 65.00
MOTHER'S DAY — 8", #10380–10382, 1995, three hair colors, Special Occasions 60.00
MOUSKETEER — 8" (see Disney under Special Events/Exclusives)
MR. AND MRS. FRANKENSTEIN SET — 8", 1996 . . . . .155.00

Mr. O'Hara — 8", #638, 1993 only, Scarlett Series (Wendy) 125.00
Mrs. Buck Rabbit — Cloth/felt, mid-1930s 625.00
Mrs. Claus — (see mid-year specials for Madame Alexander Co.under Special Events/Exclusives)
    14", #24607, 1995, Christmas Series 100.00
Mrs. Darling — 10", 1993–1994, Peter Pan Series (Cissette) 125.00
Mrs. Fezziwig — 8", #18005, 1996, Dickens, moiré gown 60.00
Mrs. March Hare — Cloth/felt, mid-1930s 625.00
Mrs. Malloy's Millinery Shop — 10" Portrette, #201167, 1995 only, trunk set with wardrobe and hats 250.00
Mrs. O'Hara — 8", #638, 1992–1993 only, Scarlett Series (Wendy) .125.00
Mrs. Quack-a-field — Cloth/felt, mid-1930s 625.00
Mrs. Snoopie — Cloth/felt, 1940s 625.00
Muffin — 19" cloth, 1966 only 125.00
    14", 1963–1977 . . . . .95.00
    14" cloth, 1965 only, sapphire eyes 95.00
    14" black cloth, 1965–1966 only 125.00
    14" cloth, 1966–1970, cut slanted blue eyes 100.00
    14" cloth, eyes like sideways commas 75.00
    12" all vinyl, 1989–1990 (Janie) 75.00
    12", 1990–1992, in trunk/wardrobe 150.00
Munchkin Peasant — 8", #140444, 1993–1995, Wizard of Oz Series 100.00
    Herald — 8" #140445, 1994–1995, Wizard of Oz Series 90.00
    Mayor — 8", #140443, 1993–1995, Wizard of Oz Series 100.00
    Lollipop — 8", #14513, 1995, Wizard of Oz Series, pink/white striped outfit 90.00
    Lullaby — 8", #14512, 1995, Wizard of Oz Series, white gown .85.00
    Lullaby League — 8", #13300, 1999, pink dress and hat 67.00
My Doll House — (see Special Events/Exclusives)
My Little Sweetheart — (see Child At Heart under Special Events/Exclusives)
Nan McDare — Cloth/felt, 1940s 625.00

Munchkin Herald, 8", #140445, 1994 (Wendy). Wizard of Oz Series.

Mrs. O'Hara, 8", hard plastic (Wendy). 1993 only. From the Scarlett Series.

PLEASE READ "WHAT IS A PRICE GUIDE?" FOR ADDITIONAL INFORMATION

NANA — 6" dog with bonnet, #441, 1993 only, Peter Pan Series 55.00
NANA/GOVERNESS — 8" h.p., #433, 1957 only (Wendy Ann) . . . . .2,000.00 up
NANCY ANN — 17–18" h.p., 1950 only (tagged Nancy Ann) . . . . .975.00 up
NANCY DAWSON — 8", #441, 1988–1989, Storybook Series (Maggie) .75.00
NANCY DREW — 12" plastic/vinyl, 1967 only, Literature Series . . . . .325.00 up
NANCY JEAN — 8" (see Belks & Leggett under Special Events/Exclusives)
NAPOLEON — 12", #1330, 1980–1986, Portraits of History (Nancy Drew) 75.00
NAT (LITTLE MEN) — 15" h.p., 1952 (Maggie) . . . . .900.00 up
NATASHA — 21", #2255, 1989–1990, brown & paisley brocade (Jacqueline) 350.00
NATIVITY SET — 1997–1999, 19460, Mary, Joseph, Jesus, Angel creche, Three Wise Men, Shepherd, Drummer . . .950.00
NASHVILLE GOES COUNTRY — 8" (1995, see C.U. under Special Events/Exclusives)
NASHVILLE SKATER
    #1 (see Collectors United under Special Events/Exclusives)
    #2 (see Collectors United under Special Events/Exclusives)
NATIONAL VELVET — 12", 1991 only, Romance Series, no riding crop (Nancy Drew) 85.00
    8", #10409, 1996, riding habit 95.00
NEIMAN-MARCUS — (see Special Events/Exclusive
NELSON, LORD — 12" vinyl, 1336, 1984–1986, Portraits of History (Nancy Drew) 75.00
NETHERLANDS BOY — Formerly "Dutch" (Wendy)
    8" h.p., straight leg, #577, 1974–1975, marked "Alex" 75.00
    8" h.p., straight leg, #577, 1976–1989, marked "Alexander" (1985–1987) 65.00
NETHERLANDS GIRL — 8" h.p., #591, #525, 1974–1992 (Wendy) 65.00
NEW ENGLAND COLLECTOR SOCIETY — (see Special Events/Exclusives)
    NICOLE — 10", #1139, 1989–1990, Portrette, black/off white outfit (Cissette) 90.00
    NIGERIA — 8", #11552, 1995 only (also in 1994 Neiman-Marcus trunk set as KENYA) 60.00

NIGHTINGALE, FLORENCE — 14", #1598, 1986–1987,
    Classic Series 90.00
NINA BALLERINA — 7" compo., 1940 (Tiny Betty) 325.00
    9" compo., 1939–1941 (Little Betty) 350.00
    14" h.p., 1949–1951 (Margaret) . . . . .575.00 up
    17", 1949–1951 . . . . .550.00
    15" h.p., 1951, came in various colors all years
        (Margaret) 700.00
    19", 1949–1950 . . . . .850.00 up
    23", 1951 . . . . .800.00
NIXON, PAT — (see Presidents' Ladies/First Ladies Series)
    14", 1994 only 135.00
NOD — (see Dutch Lullaby)
NOEL — 12" (see New England Collector Society under Special
    Events/Exclusives)
NORMANDY — 7" compo., 1935–1938 (Tiny Betty) 275.00
NORWAY — 8" h.p., BK, #584, 1968–1972 (Wendy Ann) . . .100.00
    8" straight leg, #584, 1973–1975, marked "Alex" 75.00
    8" straight leg, #584, 1976–1987, marked
        "Alexander" (1985–1987 white face) 65.00
    8" straight leg, #11566, 1996
        International Viking costume 75.00
NORWEGIAN — 7–8" compo., 1936–1940 (Tiny Betty) 275.00
    9" compo., 1938–1939 (Little Betty) 300.00
NURSE — 16", 1930s, cloth and felt 675.00
    7" compo., 1937, 1941–1943 (Tiny Betty) 275.00
    9" compo., 1939, 1942–1943 . . . . .325.00

Napoleon and Josephine, 12", hard plastic body, vinyl head (Nancy Drew). Made from 1980 – 1986.

13–15" compo., 1936–1937 (Betty) all white outfit, Dionne nurse ......MIB – 900.00 up .....700.00 up
15" compo., 1939, 1943 (Princess Elizabeth) 550.00
14" h.p., 1948 (Maggie & Margaret) 850.00
8" h.p., #563, 1956 only, all white dress (Wendy Ann) ....650.00 up
8", #429, 1961, all white dress, comes with baby ....650.00 up
8" BKW, BK, #329, #460,#660,#624,1962–1965, wears stripe dress, comes with baby 450.00
8", #308, all white uniform, Americana Series, 1991 ....75.00
8", #17620, 1999, World War II, brown, white costume with medicine bag 70.00
NUTCRACKER — 16", #21700, 1998–1999, Clara in rose embroidered costume 195.00
NUTCRACKER PRINCE — 8", #14571, 1995, Nutcracker Series, has mask 70.00

O

•••••••••••••• PLEASE READ "WHAT IS A PRICE GUIDE?" FOR ADDITIONAL INFORMATION ••••••••••••••••

O'BRIEN, MARGARET — 14½" compo., 1946–1948 ....750.00
17", 18", 19" compo., 1946–1948 ....850.00–1,200.00
21–24" compo., 1946–1948 ....1,000.00–1,400.00 up
14½" h.p., 1949–1951 ....900.00 up
17–18" h.p., 1949–1951 ....975.00 up
21–22" h.p., 1949–1951 ....1,200.00 up
15", porcelain, #90100, white blouse, blue pinafore 133.00
OKTOBERFEST — 8" (see Collectors Unlimited under Special Events/Exclusives)
OLD FASHIONED GIRL — 13" compo., 1945–1947 (Betty) ....550.00 up
20" compo. (Betty) 700.00
20" h.p., 1948 only (Margaret) ....800.00 up
14" h.p., 1948 only (Margaret) 650.00
OLIVE OYL — 10", #20126, 1996, Timeless Legends 90.00
OLIVER TWIST — 16" cloth, 1934,
Dickens character 650.00
7" compo., 1935–1936
(Tiny Betty) 300.00
8", #472, 1992 only, Storyland Series
(Wendy Ann) 70.00
OLIVER TWISTAIL — Cloth/felt, 1930s ...650.00
ONE, TWO, BUCKLE MY SHOE — 14", #24640,
Nursery Rhymes (Louisa) ...95.00
ONYX VELVET AND LACE GALA GOWN AND COAT —
10", h.p., #22170, 1997 – 1998
(Cissette) 125.00
OPENING NIGHT — 10", #1126, 1989 only,
Portrette, gold sheath and overshirt
(Cissette) 85.00
OPHELIA — 12", 1992, Romance Collection
(Nancy Drew) 115.00
12", 1993 only (Lissy) 150.00
ORCHARD PRINCESS — 21" compo., 1939,
1946–1947, has extra makeup
(Wendy Ann) ....2,400.00 up
ORPHANT ANNIE — 14" plastic/vinyl, #1480,
1965–1966 only, Literature Series
(Mary Ann) 325.00
#1485, 1965 only, in window box with
wardrobe ....500.00 up

Margaret O'Brien, 21", composition, 1946, all original.

PAKISTAN — 8" h.p., #532, 1993 only 65.00
PAMELA — 12" h.p., 1962–1963 only, takes wigs, excellent condition, doll only (Lissy) ....375.00 up
    12" h.p. in case, 1962–1963 ....1,000.00 up
    12" h.p. in window box, 1962–1963 ....1,000.00 up
    12" plastic/vinyl, 1969–1971, doll only (Nancy Drew) 225.00
    12" plastic/vinyl in case, 1969 ....575.00 up
PAMELA PLAYS DRESS UP — 12" (see Horchow under Special Events/Exclusives)
PAN AMERICAN – (POLLERA) — 7" compo., 1936–1938 (Tiny Betty) 300.00
PANAMA — 8", #555, 1985–1987 ....65.00
PANDORA — 8" (see Dolls 'n Bearland under Special Events/Exclusives)
PARK AVENUE ALEX THE BELLHOP — 8", h.p., #31180, 1997 – 1999, burgundy uniform 80.00
PARK AVENUE WENDY — 8", h.p., #31060, 1997 – 1999, black and white ensemble 80.00
PARLOUR MAID — 8" h.p., #579, 1956 only (Wendy Ann) ....950.00 up
PARTY SUN DRESS — 8", h.p., #344, 1957, BKW, blue or red dress with gold accents (Wendy Ann) .....475.00 up
PAT-A-CAKE — 8", #12812, 1995, floral dress with white apron and chef's hat, Nursery Rhymes Series 65.00
PATCHITY PAM & PEPPER — 15" cloth, 1965–1966 ....175.00
PATTERSON, MARTHA JOHNSON — 1982–1984, 3rd set Presidents' Ladies/First Ladies Series (Martha) 125.00
PATTY — 18" plastic/vinyl, 1965 only 275.00
PATTY PIGTAILS — 14" h.p., 1949 only (Margaret) ....675.00 up
PAULETTE — 10", #1128, 1989–1990 only, Portrette, dressed in pink velvet (Cissette) 125.00
PEACHTREE LANE — 8" in blue and 14" **SCARLETT** in green/white stripes, #16551, limited to 2,500 ....275.00 set
PEARL (JUNE) — 10", #1150, 1992 only, Birthstone Collection, white/silver flapper doll 75.00
PEASANT — 7" compo., 1936–1937 (Tiny Betty) 275.00
    9" compo., 1938–1939 (Little Betty) 300.00
PEGGY BRIDE — 14–18" h.p., 1950–1951, very blonde hair (Margaret) 950.00–1,200.00
    21" h.p., 1950 ....1,200.00 up

Peru, 8", #556 (Wendy). Made in 1986 and 1987 only.

Peter Pan set, L. to R. Tinker Bell (Cissette), Wendy (Mary Ann), Michael (Janie), and Peter Pan (Mary Ann). 1969 only.

Party Sun Dress, 8", #344, 1957 (Wendy). BK Walker. Blue cotton dress and hat accented with gold. Tagged: "Alexander-Kins."

PENNY — 34" cloth/vinyl, 1951 only . . . . .500.00 up
    42", 1951 only 800.00
    7" compo., 1938–1940 (Tiny Betty) 250.00
PEPPERMINT TWIST — 8", #14591, 1995, pink skirt and jacket in 1950s style, Nostalgia Series . . .60.00
PERSIA — 7" compo., 1936–1938 (Tiny Betty) 300.00
PERU — 8", #556, 1986–1987 . . . . .85.00
    8" h.p., #531, 1993 only (Wendy Ann) 70.00
PERUVIAN BOY — 8" h.p., BK, #770, 1965–1966 (Wendy Ann) 450.00
    8" h.p., BKW, #770 . . . . .450.00
PETER PAN — 15" h.p., 1953–1954 (Margaret) . . . . .750.00 up
    8" h.p., #310, 1953–1954 (Wendy Ann) Quiz-kin . . . . .850.00 up
    8" h.p., #465, reintroduced 1991–1993, #140465 in 1994, Storyland Series (Wendy Ann) 75.00
    8" h.p., #13660, 1999, green costume with Tinker Bell pin and sword 70.00
    14" plastic/vinyl, #1410, 1969 only (Mary Ann) 250.00
        1969 only, complete set of 4 dolls –
        Peter, Michael (12" Jamie), Wendy (14" Mary Ann), Tinker Bell (10" Cissette) . . . . .1,000.00 up
PETER PAN'S WENDY — 8", #13670, 1999, blue gown and fuzzy shoes 60.00
PHILIPPINES — 8" straight leg, #554, 1986–1987 (blue gown) 100.00
    1987, #531, dressed in yellow gown 150.00
PICNIC DAY — 18" h.p., #2001C, 1953 only, Glamour Girl Series, leaves on pink or blue print dress
    (Margaret) . . . . .1,500.00 up
PIERCE, JANE — 1982–1984, 3rd set Presidents' Ladies/First Ladies Series (Mary Ann) 125.00
PIERROT CLOWN — (see Clowns, 8" and 14")
PILGRIM — 7" compo., 1935–1938 (Tiny Betty) 275.00
    8" h.p., #100349, 1994, Americana Series 55.00
    8", #10349, 1995, Special Occasions Series 55.00
PINK CHAMPAGNE (ARLENE DAHL) — 18" h.p., red hair/pink lace/rhinestone bodice gown . . . . .5,500.00 up
PINK SPARKLE PRINCESS — 15", #22670, 1999, porcelain, pink gown 170.00
PINKIE — 12" plastic/vinyl, 1975–1987, Portrait Children (Nancy Drew) 75.00
    8", 1997 – 1998, #22120, chiffon gown, pink hat 70.00
PINKY — 16" cloth, 1940s 475.00
    23" compo./cloth baby, 1937–1939 . . . . .300.00
    13–19" vinyl baby, #3561, #5461, 1954 only, one-piece vinyl body and legs 100.00–150.00
PINOCCHIO — 8", #477, 1992–1993, Storyland Series (Wendy Ann) #140477, 1994 . . . . .80.00
PIP — All cloth, early 1930s, Dickens character 800.00
    7" compo., 1935–1936 (Tiny Betty) 300.00
PIPPI LONGSTOCKING — 18", #16003, 1996, Rag Dolls (cloth doll) . . . . Not available for sale
PISCES — 8", #21320, 1998, blue fish costume 90.00
PITTY PAT — 16" cloth, 1950s 475.00
PITTY PAT CLOWN — 1950s 450.00
PLACE IN THE SUN, A — 10", #24624, lavender ball gown 110.00
PLAYMATES — 29" cloth, 1940s . . . . .450.00 up
POCAHONTAS — 8" h.p., BK, #721, 1967–1970, Americana & Storyland Series, has baby (Wendy Ann) 425.00
    8" h.p., #318, 1991–1992, Americana Series (Wendy Ann) 75.00
    8" h.p., #100350, 1994—1995, Americana & Favorite Book Series (Wendy Ann) 55.00
    14", #24613, 1995, first dark skin doll this size, Favorite Books Series (Louisa) 90.00
POLISH (POLAND) — 7" compo., 1935–1936 (Tiny Betty) 275.00
    8" h.p., BKW, #780, 1964–1965 (Wendy Ann) 125.00
    8" BKW, #780, 1965 only (Maggie Mixup) 150.00
    8" h.p., BK, #780, 1965–1972 . . . . .100.00
    8" h.p., straight leg, #0780, #580, 1973–1975, marked "ALEX" .75.00
    8" straight leg, #580, 1976–1988 (1985–1987 white face), marked "Alexander" 65.00
    8", #523, reintroduced 1992–1993 (Maggie Mixup) 1994, #110523 . . . . .60.00
POLK, SARAH — 1979–1981, 2nd set Presidents' Ladies/First Ladies Series (Martha) 135.00
POLLERA (PAN AMERICAN) — 7" compo., 1936–1938 (Tiny Betty) 275.00
POLLY — 17" plastic/vinyl, 1965 only, dressed in ballgown 375.00
    Dressed in street dress 275.00
    Dressed as ballerina 275.00

P

P

Dressed as bride 300.00

1965 only, came in trunk with wardrobe . . . . .750.00 up

POLLY FLINDERS — 8", #443, 1988–1989, Storybook Series (Maggie) .80.00

POLLY PIGTAILS — 14½" h.p., 1949–1951 (Maggie) 500.00

17–17½", 1949–1951 . . . . .625.00

8" (see M.A.D.C. under Special Events/Exclusives)

POLLY PUT KETTLE ON — 7" compo., 1937–1939 (Tiny Betty) 275.00

8", h.p., #11640, 1998–1999, teacup print dress, kettle 80.00

POLLYANA — 16" rigid vinyl, 1960–1961, marked "1958" (Marybel) 425.00

16", dressed in formal 450.00

22", 1960–1961 . . . . .500.00

14", #1588, 1987–1988, Classic Series (Mary Ann) 90.00

14", reintroduced 1994 only, #24159 . . . . .100.00

8", #474, 1992–1993 only, Storyland Series (Wendy) 85.00

POODLES — 14–17", early 1950s, standing or sitting, named **IVY, PIERRE,** and **FIFI** . . . . .400.00 up

POOR CINDERELLA — (see Cinderella)

POPEYE — 8", #10428, 1996, Timeless Legends 85.00

POPEYE, OLIVE OYL, AND SWEET PEA — #20127, 1996 . . . . .175.00 set

POPPY — 9" early vinyl, 1953 only, orange organdy dress & bonnet 95.00

PORTRAIT ELISE — 17" plastic/vinyl, 1972–1973 . . . . .225.00

PORTUGAL — 8" h.p., BK, #785, 1968–1972 (Wendy Ann) 100.00

8" straight leg, #0785, #585, 1973–1975, marked "Alex" 75.00

8" straight leg, #585, #537, 1976–1987, marked "Alexander" 65.00

8", #537, 1986, white face 60.00

8" h.p., #535, 1993, #110535, 1994 . . . . .55.00

POSEY PET — 15" cloth, 1940s, plush rabbit or other animals, must be clean 450.00

PRECIOUS — 12" compo./cloth baby, 1937–1940 . . . . .275.00

12" all h.p. toddler, 1948–1951 . . . . .350.00

PREMIER DOLLS — 8" (see M.A.D.C. under Special Events/Exclusives)

PRESIDENTS' LADIES/FIRST LADIES —

1st set, 1976–1978 . . . . .150.00–175.00 singles . . . . 1,000.00 set

2nd set, 1979–1981 . . . . .125.00 singles . . . . . 800.00 set

3rd set, 1982–1984 . . . . .125.00 singles . . . . . 800.00 set

4th set, 1985–1987 . . . . .125.00 singles . . . . . 700.00 set

5th set, 1988 . . . . .125.00 singles . . . . . 700.00 set

6th set, 1989–1990 . . . . .125.00 singles . . . . . 700.00 set

PRINCE CHARLES — 8" h.p., #397, 1957 only (Wendy Ann) . . . . .750.00 up

PRINCE CHARMING — 16–17" compo., 1947 (Margaret) 800.00

14–15" h.p., 1948–1950 (Margaret) 700.00

17–18" h.p., 1948–1950 (Margaret) 850.00

21" h.p., 1949–1951 (Margaret) . . . . .1,000.00 up

12", 1990–1991, Romance Collection (Nancy Drew) 85.00

8", #479, 1993, Storybook Series, royal blue/gold outfit 80.00

8", #14541, 1995, Brothers Grimm Series, braid trimmed jacket with brocade vest 70.00

PRINCE PHILLIP — 17–18" h.p., 1953 only, Beaux Arts Series (Margaret) . . . . .850.00 up

21", 1953 only . . . . .975.00 up

PRINCESS — 12", 1990–1991 only, Romance Collection (Nancy Drew) 95.00

14", #1537, 1990 - Mary Ann; 1991 - Jennifer, Classic Series 100.00

20" h.p., 1955 only, Child's Dream Comes True Series (Cissy) . . . . .1,000.00 up

PRINCESS ALEXANDRIA — 24" cloth/compo., 1937 only . . . . .300.00 up

PRINCESS ANN — 8" h.p., #396, 1957 only (Wendy Ann) . . . . .800.00 up

PRINCESS BUDIR AL-BUDOR — 8", #483, 1993–1994 only, Storybook Series 65.00

PRINCESS DIANA BIRTHDAY — 10", white satin and gold gown 170.00

PRINCESS DOLL — 13–15" compo., 1940–1942 (Princess Elizabeth) . . . . .550.00 up

24" compo., 1940–1942 (Princess Elizabeth) . . . . .850.00 up

PRINCESS ELIZABETH — 7" compo., 1937–1939 (Tiny Betty) 350.00

8", 1937, with Dionne head (**rare**) 400.00

9–11" compo., 1937–1941 (Little Betty) 375.00–425.00
13" compo., 1937–1941, with closed mouth (Betty) . . . . .625.00 up
14" compo., 1937–1941 . . . . .600.00 up
15" compo., open mouth . . . . .600.00 up
18–19" compo., 1937–1941, open mouth 750.00
24" compo., 1938–1939, open mouth . . . . .900.00 up
28" compo., 1938–1939, open mouth . . . . .1,000.00 up
PRINCESS DIANA — 10", #22500, 1998 (Cissette), white satin gown 175.00
PRINCESS FLAVIA (ALSO VICTORIA) — 21" compo., 1939, 1946–1947 (Wendy Ann) . . . . .2,000.00 up
PRINCESS MARGARET ROSE — 15–18" compo., 1937–1938 (Princess Elizabeth) . . . . .800.00 up
21" compo., 1938 . . . . .975.00
14–18" h.p., 1949–1953 (Margaret) 650.00–975.00
18" h.p. #2020B, 1953 only, Beaux Arts Series, pink taffeta gown w/ red ribbon, tiara (Margaret) 1,700.00 up
PRINCESS ROSETTA — 21" compo., 1939, 1946–1947 (Wendy Ann) 2,300.00
PRISTINE ANGEL — 10", #10604, 100th Anniversary, second in series, white/gold 95.00
PRISCILLA — 18" cloth, mid 1930s 625.00
7" compo., 1935–1938 (Tiny Betty) 275.00
8" h.p., BK, #729, 1965–1970, Americana & Storybook Series (Wendy Ann) 325.00
PRISSY — 8", #630, 1990 only, Scarlett Series (Wendy Ann) 100.00
8", #637, reintroduced 1992–1993 . . . . .95.00
8", #16650, 1995, Scarlett Series, floral gown 80.00
PROM QUEEN (MEMORIES) — 8" (see M.A.D.C. under Special Events/Exclusives)
PSYCHO — 10", #14810, doll in shower, pictured 1998 catalog . . . . .Not available for sale
PUDDIN' — 14–21" cloth/vinyl, 1966–1975 . . . . .85.00
14–18", 1987 . . . . .75.00–95.00
14–21", 1990–1993 . . . . .75.00–125.00
14" only, 1994–1995 . . . . .85.00
21", 1995 . . . . .100.00
PUERTO RICO — 8", 1998–1999, #24120, red outfit, carries flag and frog 80.00
PUMPKIN — 22" cloth/vinyl, 1967–1976 . . . . .125.00
22", 1976 only, with rooted hair 150.00
PUPPET, HAND (ALSO SEE MARIONETTES) — Compo. head, cloth hand mitt body, by Tony Sarg, ca. 1936 . .475.00 up
PUSS 'N BOOTS — 8", #14552, Fairy Tales Series 65.00

Betty Taylor Bliss, 14", #1512 (Mary Ann). From the second set of First Ladies. Made from 1979 – 1981.

Portugal, 8" (Wendy). Made from 1968 – 1986.

PUSSY CAT — Cloth/vinyl.

WHITE DOLLS:

14", 1965–1985 (20 year production) 65.00

14", 1987–1995 . . . . .65.00

14", 1966, 1968, in trunk/trousseau . . . . .250.00 up

18", 1989–1995 . . . . .100.00

20", 1965–1984, 1987–1988 (20+ year production) 100.00

24", 1965–1985 (20 year production) 125.00

14", 1998, variety of outfits 75.00–90.00

BLACK DOLLS:

14", 1970–1976 . . . . .75.00

14", 1984–1995 (12 year production) 75.00

20", 1976–1983 . . . . .125.00

PUSSY CAT, LIVELY — 14", 20", 24", 1966–1969 only, knob makes head & limbs move 75.00–175.00

. . . . PLEASE READ "WHAT IS A PRICE GUIDE?" FOR ADDITIONAL INFORMATION . . . .

QUEEN — 18" h.p., #2025, 1953 only, Beaux Arts Series, white gown, long velvet cape trimmed with fur (Margaret) 1,800.00

18" h.p., 1953 only, Glamour Girl Series, same gown/tiara as above but no cape (Margaret) 1,400.00

18" h.p., 1954 only, Me & My Shadow Series, white gown, short Orlon cape (Margaret) 1,200.00

8" h.p., 1954, #0030C, #597, Me & My Shadow Series, Orlon cape attached to purple robe (Wendy Ann) . . . . .1,000.00 up

8", #499, 1955 only, scarlet velvet robe 750.00

10" h.p., #971, #879, #842, #763, 1957–1958, 1960–1961, gold gown with blue ribbon 425.00

#742, #765, 1959, 1963, white gown with blue ribbon 425.00

#1186, #1187, 1972–1973, white gown with red ribbon 350.00

1959, in trunk with wardrobe, must be mint . . . . .950.00 up

14", #1536, 1990 only, Classic Series (Louisa, Jennifer) 90.00

20" h.p./vinyl arms, 1955, Dreams Come True Series, white brocade gown (Cissy) . . . . .1,200.00 up

1957, Fashion Parade Series, white gown 950.00

1958, 1961–1963 (1958 - Dolls To Remember Series), gold gown 900.00

Cissette Queen, #971, 1957. All original and mint. Tagged: "Cissette."

Queen Elizabeth II, 17", #1780, 1963. A full jointed plastic doll with joints at the ankles for high heels. Brocade gown with the sash of the order of the Bath.

18", 1963 only, white gown with red ribbon (Elise) 750.00
   With vinyl head (Marybel) 875.00
18" vinyl, same as 1965 (21" with rooted hair, 1966 only), gold brocade gown, rare doll (Elise) 975.00
#2150, 21" h.p./vinyl arms, 1965, white brocade gown (Jacqueline) 750.00
   1968, gold gown 750.00
QUEEN ALEXANDRINE — 21" compo., 1939–1941 (Wendy Ann) .1,975.00
QUEEN CHARLOTTE — 10" (see M.A.D.C. under Special Events/Exclusives)
QUEEN ELIZABETH I — 10" (see My Doll House under Special Events/Exclusives)
        8", #12610, 1999, red velvet trimmed in gold 85.00
QUEEN ELIZABETH II — 8", 1992 only (mid-year issue), commemorating reign's 40th anniversary 150.00
QUEEN ESTHER — 8", #14584, 1995 only, Bible Series 100.00
QUEEN OF HEARTS — 8" straight leg, #424, 1987–1990, Storybook Series (Wendy Ann) 75.00
   8", #14511, 1995, Alice In Wonderland Series 75.00
   10" (see Disney under Special Events/Exclusives)
QUEEN ISABELLA — 8" h.p., #329, 1992 only, Americana Series .125.00
QUEEN OF THE ROSES — 10", #22660, 1999, yellow satin long dress 110.00
QUINTUPLETS (FISCHER QUINTS) — 7", h.p. & vinyl 1964 (Genius) . . . . .550.00 set
QUIZ-KINS — 8" h.p., 1953, bald head, in romper only (Wendy Ann) . . . . .475.00 up
   1953 Peter Pan, caracul wig 850.00
   1953–1954, as groom . . . . .600.00 up
   1953–1954, as bride . . . . .650.00 up
   1953–1954, girl with wig, ...650.00 up
   1953, girl without wig, in romper suit 550.00

R

• • • • • • • • • • • • • • PLEASE READ "WHAT IS A PRICE GUIDE?" FOR ADDITIONAL INFORMATION • • • • • • • • • • • • • • • •

RACHEL/RACHAEL — 8", 1989 (see Belks & Leggett under Special Events/Exclusives)
RANDOLPH, MARTHA — 1976–1978, 1st set Presidents' Ladies/First Ladies Series (Louisa) 150.00
RAPUNZEL — 10", #M31, 1989–1992 only, Portrette, gold velvet (Cissette) .125.00
   14", #1539, 1993–1994, Doll Classics, limited to 3,000, comes with 8" Mother Gothel 250.00
   14", #87005, 1996, purple gown (Louisa) 125.00
   8", #14542, 1995, Brothers Grimm Series, pink gown with gold scallops,
      #13980, 1997–1999 . . . . .75.00
REALLY UGLY STEPSISTER — 8", h.p., #13450, 1997 – 1998,
   Cinderella Series 85.00
REBECCA — 14–17", 21" compo., 1940–1941
   (Wendy Ann) . . . . .600.00–1,000.00 up
   14" h.p., 1948–1949 (Margaret) . . . . .850.00 up
   14" plastic/vinyl, #1485, 1968–1969, Classic Series,
     two-tiered skirt in pink (Mary Ann) 175.00
      #1485, #1515, #1585, 1970–1985, one-piece skirt,
     pink pindot or check dress 85.00
      #1586, 1986–1987, blue dress with striped pinafore 85.00
   8", #14647, 1996 . . . . .65.00
RECORD ALBUM — "Madame Alexander Collector's Album," 1978,
   Children's stories told by Madame.
   Cover is like Alexander box 35.00
RED BOY — 8" h.p., BK, #740, 1972 (Wendy) 125.00
   #0740, 1973–1975, marked "Alex" 75.00
   #440, 1976–1988, marked "Alexander" 65.00
RED CROSS NURSE — 18", #16002, Rag Doll Series . . . .Not available for sale
RED RIDING HOOD — 7" compo., 1936–1942 (Tiny Betty) 275.00
   9" compo., 1939–1940 (Little Betty) 300.00

Rebecca, 14", #1586, plastic/vinyl (Mary Ann). Made from 1986 – 1987

8" h.p., SLW, #608, 1955, cape sewn under arms (Wendy Ann) 575.00
8" h.p., BKW, #382, 1962–1965, Storybook Series (Wendy Ann) 275.00
8" h.p., BK, #782, 1965–1972 . . . . .125.00
8" h.p., straight leg, #0782, #482, 1973–1975, marked "Alex" 75.00
8" h.p., straight leg, #482, 1976–1986 (1985–1987 white face), marked "Alexander" 65.00
8", #485, #463, 1987–1991 (Maggie), 1992–1993 (Wendy Ann), #140463,1994, #13970,1998–1999 . . . .65.00
14", #24617, 1995, patchwork dress with red cape (Mary Ann) 100.00
14", #87004, plaid dress with red cape (Mary Ann) 75.00
RED SHOES — 8", #14533, 1995, ballerina with same head as **SPAIN** 70.00
RED QUEEN — 8", h.p., 1997–1999, #13010, red and gold gown 120.00
RED QUEEN AND WHITE KING SET — 8" pair, #13030, 1997 . . . . .210.00
RED SEQUIN — 10", #19974, 1998 (Cissette), long red velvet 160.00
RENOIR — 21" compo., 1945–1946, extra makeup, must be excellent (Wendy Ann) . . . . .2,000.00 up
14" h.p., 1950 only (Margaret) . . . . .875.00 up
21" h.p./vinyl arms, 1961 only (Cissy) . . . . .825.00 up
18" h.p./vinyl arms, vinyl head, 1963 only (Elise) . . . . .575.00 up
#2154, 21" h.p./vinyl arms, 1965, pink gown (Jacqueline) 700.00
#2062, 1966, blue gown with black trim (Coco) 2,200.00
#2175, 1967, navy blue gown, red hat 750.00
#2194, #2184, 1969–1970, blue gown, full lace overdress 650.00
#2163, 1971, all yellow gown 650.00
#2190, 1972, pink gown with black jacket & trim 550.00
#2190, 1973, yellow gold gown, black ribbon 550.00
10" h.p., #1175, 1968, all navy with red hat (Cissette) 475.00
#1175, 1969, pale blue gown, short jacket, stripe or dotted skirt 475.00
#1180, 1970, all aqua satin 425.00
RENOIR CHILD — 12" plastic/vinyl, #1274, 1967 only, Portrait Children Series (Nancy Drew) 150.00
14", #1474, 1968 only (Mary Ann) 175.00
RENOIR GIRL — 14" plastic/vinyl, #1469, #1475, 1967–1968, Portrait Children Series, white dress with
    red ribbon trim (Mary Ann) 195.00
#1477, 1969–1971, pink dress, white pinafore 100.00
#1477, #1478, #1578, 1972–1986 (14 year production), pink multi-tiered lace gown 95.00

Renoir, 21", #2190, 1973 (Jacqueline).

Renoir Girl, 14" (Mary Ann), plastic/vinyl. Left: #1477, 1969 only. Right: #1477, 1970 – 1971.

#1572, 1986 only, pink pleated nylon dress 75.00
RENOIR GIRL WITH WATERING CAN — #1577, 1985–1987, Classic & Fine Arts Series 100.00
8", h.p., #22150, 1997, navy taffeta dress 75.00
RENOIR GIRL WITH HOOP — #1574, 1986–1987, Classic & Fine Arts Series 95.00
RENOIR MOTHER — 21" h.p./vinyl arms, 1967 only, navy blue, red hat (Jacqueline) . . . . .900.00 up
RENOIR'S ON THE TERRACE — 8", 1999 (Wendy) blue dress with white overdress 80.00
RHETT — 12", #1380, 1981–1985, Portrait Children Series, black jacket/grey pants (Nancy Drew) 85.00
8", #401, 1989 only, Jubilee II (Wendy Ann) 100.00
8", #632, #642, 1991–1992 only, Scarlett Series, all white/blue vest 85.00
8", #642, 1993, #160642, 1994, tan pants/vest/tie with white jacket 80.00
10", h.p., #15050, 1997, *Gone with the Wind* Series 95.00
RIDING HABIT — 8", 1990 only, Americana Series (Wendy Ann) 75.00
#571, 1956 . . . . .500.00
#373G, 1957 . . . . .475.00
#541, 1958 . . . . .550.00
#355, 1962 . . . . .385.00
#623, 1965 . . . . .350.00
RILEY'S LITTLE ANNIE — 14" plastic/vinyl, #1481, 1967 only, Literature Series (Mary Ann) 250.00
RING AROUND THE ROSEY — 8", #12813, Nursery Rhymes Series 60.00
8", #13520, 1998–1999, pink and white lacey dress 80.00
RINGBEARER — 14" h.p., 1951 only, must be near mint (Lovey Dove) .550.00 up
RINGMASTER — 8" (see Collectors United under Special Events/Exclusives)
RIVERBOAT QUEEN (LENA) — (see M.A.D.C. under Special Events/Exclusives)
RIVIERA NIGHT — 16", print dress, matching hat 170.00
ROARING 20'S BRIDE — 10", #22630, 1999, white lace, pink roses 150.00
ROARING 20'S CATHERINE — 16", porcelain, blue satin fringed costume 215.00
ROBIN HOOD — 8", #446, 1988–1990, Storybook Series (Wendy Ann) 65.00
ROCK AND ROLL GROUP — #22110, 1997, four 8" dolls, mod costumes 300.00
ROCOCO BRIDE — 10", pink satin and lace gown 140.00
ROCOCO CATHERINE — 16", porcelain, elaborate pink satin gown 300.00
RODEO — 8" h.p., #483, 1955 only (Wendy Ann) . . . . .850.00 up
RODEO ROSIE — 14", #87012, 1996, red checked western costume 125.00
ROGERS, GINGER — 14–21" compo., 1940–1945 (Wendy Ann) . . . . .2,500.00 up
ROLLER BLADES — 8", "Throughly Modern Wendy" (see Disney under Special Events/Exclusives)
ROLLER SKATING — 8" h.p., SL, SLW, BK, #556, 1953–1956 (Wendy Ann) . . . . .550.00 up
ROMANCE — 21" compo., 1945–1946, extra makeup, must be mint (Wendy Ann) 2,100.00
ROMEO — 18" compo., 1949 (Wendy Ann) . . . . .1,500.00 up
8" h.p., #474, 1955 only (Wendy Ann) . . . . .950.00 up
12" plastic/vinyl, #1370, 1978–1987, Portrait Children Series (Nancy Drew) 75.00
12", reintroduced 1991–1992 only, Romance Collection (Nancy Drew) 80.00
8", 1994, mid-year introduction (see M.A.D.C. under Special Events/Exclusives) 125.00
ROOSEVELT, EDITH — 1988, 5th set Presidents' Ladies/First Ladies Series (Louisa) 125.00
ROOSEVELT, ELEANOR — 14", 1989–1990, 6th set Presidents' Ladies/First Ladies Series (Louisa) 135.00
ROSAMUND BRIDESMAID — 15" h.p., 1951 only (Margaret, Maggie) . . . . .500.00 up
17–18" h.p., 1951 only (Margaret, Maggie) . . . . .600.00 up
ROSE — 9" early vinyl toddler, 1953 only, pink organdy dress & bonnet 125.00
ROSEBUD — 16–19" cloth/vinyl, 1952–1953 . . . . .150.00
13", 1953 only 175.00
23–25", 1953 only 175.00
ROSEBUD (PUSSY CAT) — 14"–20", 1986 only, white 50.00
14", black 75.00
ROSE FAIRY — 8" h.p., #622, 1956 only (Wendy Ann) . . . . .1,400.00 up
8", #22640, 1999, yellow and rose costume with wings 80.00
ROSETTE — 10", #1115, 1987–1989, Portrette, pink/rose gown (Cissette) .100.00
ROSEY POSEY — 14" cloth/vinyl, 1976 only 75.00
21" cloth/vinyl, 1976 only 100.00
ROSIE THE RIVETER — 8", #17530, 1999, overalls, lunch bucket 80.00

R

Russian, 9" composition, 1935–1938. Original clothes. Tagged: "Madame Alexander"

Ross, Betsy — 8" h.p., Americana Series, 1967–1972 (Wendy Ann)
 Bend knees, #731 ....125.00
 Straight legs, #0731, #431, 1973–1975, Storybook Series,
  marked "Alex" 75.00
 Straight legs, #431, 1976–1987 (1985–1987 white face) 65.00
 8", #312, reintroduced 1991–1992 only,
  Americana Series 60.00
 #312, 1976 Bicentennial gown (star print) 125.00
Rosy — 14", #1562, 1988–1990, Classic Series, all pink dress with
  cream lace trim (Mary Ann) 85.00
Round Up Cowgirl — 8" (see Disney under Special Events/Exclusives)
Row, Row, Row Your Boat — 8", #13510, 1998–1999,
  comes with boat 100.00
Roxanne — 8" h.p., #140504, 1994 only, Storyland Series 75.00
Royal Evening — 18" h.p., 1953 only, cream/royal blue gown
  (Margaret) ....2,400.00 up
Royal Wedding — 21" compo., 1947, full circles trimmed in
  lace on lower skirt (Wendy Ann) 3,250.00
Rozy — 12" plastic/vinyl, #1130, 1969 only (Janie) 375.00
Ruby (July) — 10", #1151, 1992 only, Birthstone Collection,
  all red/gold (Cissette) 95.00
Ruffles Clown — 21", 1954 only 425.00
Rumania — 8" h.p., BK, #786, 1968–1972 (Wendy) 100.00
 8" straight leg, #0786, #586, 1973–1975, marked "Alex" ..75.00
 8" straight leg, #586, #538, 1976–1987,
  marked "Alexander" 65.00
 8", #538, 1986–1987 ....55.00
Rumbera/Rumbero — 7" compo., 1938–1943 (Tiny Betty) .350.00 each
 9" compo., 1939–1941 (Little Betty) ....375.00 each
Rumpelstiltskin & Miller's Daughter — 8" & 14", #1569, 1992 only, limited to 3,000 sets ....300.00 set
Russia — 8" h.p., BK, #774, 1968–1972 (Wendy Ann) 100.00
 8" straight leg, #0774, 1973–1975, marked "Alex" 75.00
 8" straight leg, #574, #548, 1976–1988 (1985–1987 white face), marked "Alexander" 60.00
 8", #548, 1985–1987, white face 60.00
 8", #581, 1991–1992 only 55.00
 8", #110540, 1994 only, long blue gown with gold trim 55.00
 8", #24150, 1999, comes with painted stacking doll and miniature doll 150.00
Russian — 7" compo., 1935–1938 (Tiny Betty) 285.00
 9" compo., 1938–1942 (Little Betty) 300.00
Rusty — 20" cloth/vinyl, 1967–1968 only 300.00

S

·············· PLEASE READ "WHAT IS A PRICE GUIDE?" FOR ADDITIONAL INFORMATION ··············

Sagittarius — 8", #21410, 1998 (Maggie), horse costume 90.00
Sailor — 14" compo., 1942–1945 (Wendy Ann) 750.00
 17" compo., 1943–1944 ....875.00
 8" boy, 1990 (see U.F.D.C. under Special Events/Exclusives)
 8" boy, 1991 (see FAO Schwarz under Special Events/Exclusives)
 Columbian Sailor — (see U.F.D.C. under Special Events/Exclusives)
Sailorette — 10" h.p., #1119, 1988 only, Portrette Series, red/white/blue outfit (Cissette) 75.00
Sally Bride — 14" compo., 1938–1939 (Wendy Ann) ....475.00 up
 18–21" compo., 1938–1939 ....475.00–625.00
Salome — 14", #1412, 1984–1986, Opera Series (Mary Ann) 90.00

SALUTE TO THE CENTURY — 8", #17630, 1999, white chiffon long gown 100.00
SAMANTHA — 14" 1989 (see FAO Schwarz under Special Events/Exclusives)
   14", #1561, 1991–1992 only, Classic Series, gold ruffled gown (Mary Ann) 175.00
   10", h.p., #15300, from the *Bewitched* TV series 105.00
SAMSON — 8", #14582, 1995 only, Bible Series 100.00
SANDY MCHARE — Cloth/felt, 1930s 675.00
SANTA CLAUS — 14", #24608, 1995, Christmas Series 100.00
SANTA AND MRS. CLAUS — 8", mid-year issue (see Madame Alexander Doll Co. under Special Events/Exclusives)
SANTA'S LITTLE HELPER — 8", #19660, 1998–1999, elf with candy cane trim 105.00
SAPPHIRE (SEPTEMBER) — 10", 1992 only, Birthstone Collection 95.00
SARDINIA — 8", #509, 1989–1991 only (Wendy Ann) 65.00
SARGENT — 14", #1576, 1984–1985, Fine Arts Series, dressed in lavender (Mary Ann) 85.00
SARGENT'S GIRL — 14", #1579, 1986 only, Fine Arts Series, dressed in pink (Mary Ann) 85.00
SCARECROW — 8", #430, 1993, #140430, 1994–1996, Wizard of Oz Series, #13230, 1997–1999 . . . . . . .70.00
SCARLETT O'HARA — (Before movie, 1937–1938)
   7" compo., 1937–1942 (Tiny Betty) 475.00
   9" compo., 1938–1941 (Little Betty) 500.00
   11", 1937–1942 (Wendy Ann) 675.00
   14–15" compo., 1941–1943 (Wendy Ann) 750.00
   18" compo., 1939–1946 (Wendy Ann) 1,200.00
   21" compo., 1945, 1947 (Wendy Ann) 1,500.00
   14–16" h.p., 1950s (Margaret) 1,600.00
   14–16" h.p., 1950s (Maggie) 1,650.00
   20" h.p., 1950s (Margaret) . . . . .1,800.00 up
   21", 1955, blue taffeta gown w/black looped braid trim, short jacket (Cissy) . . . . .1,400.00 up
     1958, jointed arms, green velvet jacket and bonnet trimmed in light green net. rare . . . . .2,000.00 up
     1961–1962, straight arms, white organdy,
       green ribbon inserted into tiers of lace on skirt,white picture hat, *rare* . . . . .2,000.00 up
   18" h.p./vinyl arms, 1963 only, pale blue organdy w/rosebuds, straw hat (Elise) . . . . .950.00 up
   12" h.p., 1963 only, green taffeta gown and bonnet (Lissy) 1,500.00
   7½–8", 1953–1954, white gown w/red rosebuds, white lace hat (Wendy Ann) . . . . .1,400.00 up
   7½–8" h.p., #485, 1955, two layer gown, white/yellow/green trim (Wendy Ann) . . . . .1,500.00 up
   8" h.p., BKW, 1956, pink, blue,
     or yellow floral gown . . . . .1,350.00 up
   8" h.p., BKW, #431, 1957, white, lace and ribbon trim
     (dress must be mint) . . . . .1,400.00 up
   8" h.p., BK, #760, 1963 . . . . .650.00 up
   8", BK, 1965, in white or cream gown (Wendy Ann) . . .750.00 up
   8", BK, 1971 only, bright pink floral print 650.00
   8", BK, #725, 1966–1972, Americana & Storybook Series,
     floral gown 375.00
   8", #0725, #425, 1973–1991 (18 year production),
     white gown (Wendy Ann) 100.00
     Straight leg, #425, #426, 1976–1986,
       marked "Alexander" 75.00
       #426, 1987 white face, blue dot gown 225.00
     Straight leg, #426, 1988–1989, floral gown 95.00
     1986 (see M.A.D.C. under Special Events/Exclusives)
     1989, #400, Jubilee II, green velvet/gold trim 150.00
     Straight leg, #626, 1990 only, tiny floral print 100.00
     #631, 1991 only, 3-tier white gown, curly hair 85.00
     #627, 1992 only, rose floral print, oversized bonnet 100.00
     #641, 1993, white gown with green stripes and trim 85.00
     #643, 1993, #160643, 1994 (Honeymoon In New Orleans),
       trunk with wardrobe 275.00
     #160644, 1994 only, **SCARLETT BRIDE** 100.00
     #160647, 1994 only, **SCARLETT PICNIC**, green/red floral
       on white, large ruffle at hem 100.00

Scarlett O'Hara, 8", #641, 1993 only. From the Scarlett Series.

Scarlett O'Hara, 18", composition (Wendy Ann). Exquisitely beautiful face. Taffeta dress tagged: "Scarlett O'Hara." Magnolia blossoms in hair.

SCARLETT O'HARA, CONTINUED...

#16648, 1995–1996, white four-tiered organdy gown with red trim 85.00
#16652, 1995 only, floral print picnic outfit with organdy overskirt 100.00
#16553, green drapery gown, 100th Anniversary 100.00
#16653, 1996, Ashley's Farewell, maroon taffeta skirt 75.00
#17025, 1996, Tomorrow is Another Day, floral gown 85.00
#86004, 1996, Ashley's Birthday, red velvet gown 100.00
#15030, 1997–1998, Shadow, rose picnic dress 80.00
#14970, 1998–1999, Poor Scarlett, floral calico, straw hat 95.00
#15180, 1999, Sweet Sixteen, white dress, red ribbons 90.00
8" h.p., 1990, M.A.D.C. Symposium (see M.A.D.C. Special Events/Exclusives)
8", 1993, mid-year issue (see Madame Alexander Doll Co. under Special Events/Exclusives)
21" h.p./vinyl arms, #2153, 1963–1964 (became "Godey" in 1965 with blonde hair) . . . . .1,500.00 up
21" h.p./vinyl arms, 1965, #2152, green satin gown (Jacqueline) . . . . .1,900.00 up
#2061, 1966, all white gown, red sash & roses (also with plain wide lace hem; also inverted "V"
    scalloped lace hem – allow more for this gown) (Coco) . . . . .2,700.00 up
#2174, 1967, green satin gown with black trim 675.00
#2180, 1968, floral print gown with wide white hem . . . . .1,000.00 up
#2190, 1969, red gown with white lace 650.00
#2180, 1970, green satin, white trim on jacket 575.00
#2292, 2295, 2296, 1975–1977, all green satin, white lace at cuffs 450.00
#2110, 1978, silk floral gown, green parasol, white lace 500.00
#2240, 1979–1985, green velvet 350.00
#2255, 1986 only, floral gown, green parasol, white lace 375.00
#2247, 1987–1988, layered all over white gown 350.00
#2253, 1989, doll has full bangs, all red gown (Birthday Party gown) 400.00
#2258, 1990–1993 only, Scarlett Bride, Scarlett Series 350.00
#2259, 1991–1992 only, green on white, three ruffles around skirt 350.00
21" #162276, 1994 (Jacqueline) tight green gown, three layered bustle 300.00
#009, porcelain, 1991 only, green velvet, gold trim 600.00
#50001, Scarlett Picnic (Jacqueline), floral gown 325.00
#15020, 1997, rose picnic dress, carries garden basket 375.00
#15170, Black Mourning Scarlett, 1999 . . . . .500.00
10" h.p., #1174, 1968 only, lace in bonnet, green satin gown with black braid trim (Cissette) 475.00
#1174, 1969, green satin gown with white & gold braid 425.00
#1181, #1180, 1970–1973, green satin gown with gold braid trim 400.00
10" h.p., #1100, 1989 only, Jubilee II, burgundy and white 150.00
#1102, 1990–1991 only, Scarlett Series, floral print gown 175.00
10", #1105, 1992 only, Scarlett at Ball, all in black 135.00
10", 1993, #161105, 1994, green velvet drapes/gold trim 150.00
10", 1994–1995, Scarlett in red dress with red boa 150.00

10", #16107, 1995 only, white sheath with dark blue jacket 135.00
10", #16654, 1996, mourning dress 125.00
10", #16656, 1996, Scarlett and Rhett, limited set 210.00
10", #15000, 1997 – 1998, Hoop-Petti outfit 110.00
10", #15040, 1997, mourning outfit 115.00
10", #14980, 1998–1999, blue satin gown, lace shawl (Cissette) 135.00
12", 1981–1985, green gown with braid trim (Nancy Drew) 125.00
14" plastic/vinyl, #1495, 1968 only, floral gown (Mary Ann) 450.00
   #1490, #7590, 1969–1986 (18 year production), white gown,
      tagged "Gone With The Wind" (Mary Ann) 100.00
   #1590, #1591, 1987–1989, blue or green floral print on beige 140.00
   #1590, 1990, Scarlett Series, tiny floral print gown 150.00
   #1595, 1991–1992 only, Scarlett Series, white ruffles, green ribbon (Louisa, Jennifer) 140.00
   #16551, 1995 (see **PEACHTREE LANE**)
   #1500, 14", 1986 only, Jubilee #1, all green velvet (Mary Ann) 175.00
   #1300, 14", 1989 only, Jubilee #2, green floral print gown (Mary Ann) 150.00
SCARLETT, MISS —14" (see Belks & Leggett under SpecialEvents/Exclusives)
SCHOOL GIRL — 7" compo., 1936–1943 (Tiny Betty) 285.00
SCOTCH — 7" compo., 1936–1939 (Tiny Betty) 275.00
   9" compo., 1939–1940 (Little Betty) 350.00
   10" h.p., 1962–1963 (Cissette) . . . . .900.00 up
SCOTS LASS — 8" h.p., BKW, #396, 1963 only (Maggie Mixup, Wendy Ann) . . . . .275.00 up
SCORPIO — 8", #21400, 1998, Scorpion costume, golden spear 90.00
SCOTTISH (SCOTLAND) — 8" h.p., BKW, #796, 1964–1965 (Wendy Ann) .150.00
   8" h.p., BK, #796, 1965–1972 . . . . .125.00
   8" straight leg, #0796-596, 1973–1975, marked "ALEX" 85.00
   8" straight leg, #596, #529, 1976–1993 (1985–1987 white face), marked "Alexander" 70.00
   8" redressed, Scot outfit with English guard hat, 1994 . . . . .65.00
SCOUT — 8", #367, 1991–1992 only, Americana Series 95.00
SCROOGE — 14", #18401, 1990, Dickens (Mary Ann) 125.00
SEARS ROEBUCK — (see Special Events/Exclusives)
SECRET GARDEN, MY — 8" (see FAO Schwarz under Special Events/Exclusives)
   14", #24616, 1995, has trunk and wardrobe (Louisa) 225.00
SEPTEMBER — 14", #1527, 1989 only, Classic Series (Mary Ann) 85.00
   10", #1152, 1992, Portrette, royal blue/gold flapper 100.00
SEVEN DWARFS — Compo., 1937 only, must be mint . . . . .475.00 each
SEVENTY-FIFTH ANNIVERSARY WENDY — 8", #22420, 1998, pink outfit .110.00
SHADOW OF MADAME — (see Doll & Teddy Bear Expo under Special Events/Exclusives)
SHADOW STEPMOTHER — 8", #14638, 1996 . . . . .85.00
SHAHARAZAD — 10", #1144, 1992–1993 only, Portrette (Cissette) 85.00
SHE SELLS SEASHELLS — 8", #14629, 1996, Nursery Rhyme (Maggie) 75.00
SHEA ELF — 8" (see Collectors United under Special Events/Exclusives)
SHEPHERD AND DRUMMER BOY SET — 8", #19490, 1997–1999, Nativity set 160.00
SHEPHERDESS WITH LAMB — 8", #20010, 1999, red robe, headdress 85.00
SHIMMERING 30'S CATHERINE — porcelain, 16", white long gown 200.00
SHIRLEY'S DOLL HOUSE — (see Special Events/Exclusives)
SHOEMAKER'S ELF BOY — 8", #14637, 1996 . . . . .65.00
SHOEMAKER'S ELF GIRL — 8", #14636, 1996 . . . . .65.00
SICILY — 8", #513, 1989–1990 (Wendy Ann) 75.00
SIMONE — 21" h.p./vinyl arms, 1968 only, in trunk (Jacqueline) . . . . .2,150.00 up
SIR LAPIN HARE — Cloth/felt, 1930s 700.00
SISTER BRENDA — (see FAO Schwarz under Special Events/Exclusives)
SITTING PRETTY — 18" foam body, 1965 only, *rare* 400.00
SKATER'S WALTZ — 15"-18", 1955–1956 (Cissy) 650.00
SKATING DOLL — 16", 1947–1950 (untagged "Sonja Henie" after contract expired) 700.00
SLEEPING BEAUTY — 7–9" compo., 1941–1944 (Tiny Betty & Little Betty) 325.00–450.00
   15–16" compo., 1938–1940 (Princess Elizabeth) 475.00

S

　　　18–21" compo., 1941–1944 (Wendy Ann) 650.00–800.00
　　　10", #1141, 1991–1992 only, Portrette, blue/white gown 90.00
　　　21", #2195, 1959 only year this head used, authorized by Disney, blue satin brocade, net cape, gold tiara .850.00 up
　　　16" #1895, same head as 21" on Elise body, authorized by Disney 650.00
　　　10" h.p., 1959 only, authorized by Disney, blue gown (Cissette) 355.00
　　　14" plastic/vinyl, #1495, #1595, 1971–1985 (14 year production), Classic Series, gold gown (Mary Ann) 90.00
　　　14", #1596, 1986–1990, Classic Series, blue gown (Mary Ann) .120.00
　　　14", #87010, 1996, pink and gold ball gown (Mary Ann) 125.00
　　　8", #14543, 1995, Brothers Grimm Series, blue with silver crown 70.00
　　　8", #13600, 1997 – 1999, blue satin gown, spinning wheel 75.00
SLEEPING BEAUTY'S PRINCE — 8", #13650, 1999, purple costume 80.00
SLUMBERMATE — 11–12" cloth/compo., 1940s . . . . .250.00 up
　　　21" compo/cloth, 1940s . . . . .475.00 up
　　　13" vinyl/cloth, 1951 only . . . . .125.00 up
SMARTY — 12" plastic/vinyl, #1160, #1136, 1962–1963 . . . . .325.00
　　　1963 only, "Smarty & Baby" 375.00
　　　1963 only, with boy "Artie" in case with wardrobe 950.00
SMEE — 8", #442, 1993, #140442, 1994, Storybook Series (Peter Pan), wears glasses 65.00
SMILEY — 20" cloth/vinyl, 1971 only (Happy) 250.00
SMOKEY TAIL — Cloth/felt, 1930s 650.00
SNAP, CRACKLE, POP SET — 8", #12120, 1998–1999, Rice Krispies Dolls set 250.00
SNOWFLAKE — 10", #1167, 1993 only, Portrette, ballerina dressed in white/gold outfit (Cissette) 90.00
SNOWFLAKE SYMPOSIUM — (see M.A.D.C. under Special Events/Exclusives)
SNOW QUEEN — 10", #1130, 1991–1992 only, Portrette, silver/white gown (Cissette) 100.00
　　　8", #14548, Hans Christian Andersen Series, white with gold trim 70.00
SNOW WHITE — 13" compo., 1937–1939, painted eyes (Princess Elizabeth) 475.00
　　　12" compo., 1939–1940 (Princess Elizabeth) 450.00
　　　13" compo, 1939–1940, sleep eyes (Princess Elizabeth) 475.00
　　　16" compo., 1939–1942 (Princess Elizabeth) 500.00
　　　18" compo., 1939–1940 (Princess Elizabeth) 750.00

Smarty, 12", #1140, 1962, pink cotton dress with white dots. All original vinyl head with rooted hair.

　　　14–15" h.p., 1952 only (Margaret) 750.00
　　　18–23", 1952 only .850.00–1,050.00
　　　21" h.p., *rare* (Margaret) 1,200.00
　　　14", #1455, 1967–1977, Disney crest colors (Mary Ann) 350.00
　　　8" h.p., 1972–1977, Disney crest colors (Wendy) 425.00
　　　8", #495, 1990–1992 only, Storyland Series (Wendy) . . .85.00
　　　8", #14545, 1995, Brothers Grimm Series, crest colors
　　　　　but with red bodice, #13800, 1997–1999 . . . . .55.00
　　　12", 1990 (see Disney under Special Events/Exclusives)
　　　14" plastic/vinyl, #1455, #1555, 1970–1985
　　　　　(15 year production), Classic Series, white gown
　　　　　(Mary Ann) 125.00
　　　#1556, #1557, 1986–1992, ecru & gold gown, red cape
　　　　　(Mary Ann, Louisa) 150.00
　　　14", #14300, 1995, crest colors but red bodice (Louisa) 200.00
　　　14", #87013, 1996, Snow White's trunk set (Mary Ann) 325.00
　　　10", Disney crest colors (see Disney/Special Events)
SNOW WHITE'S PRINCE — 8", #14639, 1996 . . . . .65.00
SO BIG — 22" cloth/vinyl, 1968–1975, painted eyes 225.00
SOCCER BOY — 8", #16350, sports outfit
　　　with soccer ball, 1997 . . . . .60.00
SOCCER GIRL — 8", #16341, sports outfit
　　　with soccer ball, 1997 – 1998 . . . . .60.00
SO LITE BABY OR TODDLER — 20" cloth, 1930–1940s . . . . .375.00 up
SOLDIER — 14" compo., 1943–1944 (Wendy Ann) 375.00
　　　17" compo., 1942–1945 (Wendy Ann) 850.00
SOUND OF MUSIC, LARGE SET, 1965–1970
　　　14", #1404, Louisa (Mary Ann) 275.00

   10", #1107 Friedrich (Janie or Smarty) 275.00
   14", #1403 Brigitta (Mary Ann) 195.00
   14", #1405 Liesl (Mary Ann) 275.00
   10" Marta, 10" Gretl (Smarty or Janie) 195.00
   17", #1706 Maria (Elise or Polly) 300.00
   Full set of 7 dolls 1,200.00

SOUND OF MUSIC, SMALL SET, 1971–1973
   12" Maria (Nancy Drew) 325.00
   8" #801 Gretl (Wendy Ann) 175.00
   8" #802 Marta, #807 Friedrich (Wendy Ann) 225.00
   10" Brigitta (Cissette) 175.00
   10" Liesl (Cissette) 275.00
   10" Louisa (Cissette) 275.00
   Set of 7 dolls 1,250.00

SOUND OF MUSIC, DRESSED IN SAILOR SUITS & TAGGED, DATE UNKNOWN
   17" Maria (Elise or Polly) 500.00
   14" Louisa (Mary Ann) 500.00
   10" Friedrich (Smarty) 375.00
   14" Brigitta (Mary Ann) 375.00
   14" Liesl (Mary Ann) 375.00
   10" Gretl (Smarty) 350.00
   10" Marta (Smarty) 375.00
   Set of 7 dolls . . . . .2,700.00 up
   12", 1965, in sailor suit (Lissy) . . . . .750.00 up
   12", 1965, in alpine outfit (Lissy) 650.00

SOUND OF MUSIC — All in same ouﬁt: red skirt, white attached blouse,
   black vest that ties in front with gold cord, *very rare* . . . . .400.00–600.00 each

SOUND OF MUSIC, REINTRODUCED 1992–1993
   8", #390, #391, 1992–1993 only, Gretl and Kurt (boy in sailor suit) 125.00
   8", #390, #392, 1992–1994, Brigitta 100.00
   8", #394, 1993 only, Friedrich dressed in green/white playsuit 100.00
   8", #393, 1993 only, Marta in sailor dress 195.00
   10", 1992–1993 only, Maria (Cissette) 125.00
   10", 1993 only, Liesl 125.00
   12", 1992 only, Maria Bride (Nancy Drew) 125.00
   10", Maria At Abbey, dressed in nun's outfit (Cissette) 1993 only .125.00

SOUND OF MUSIC, REINTRODUCED 1998
   8", #14060, Gretl Von Trapp (Wendy), green, gray sailor suit 100.00
   8", #14050, Marta Von Trapp (Maggie), sailor suit 100.00
   9", #14040, Brigitta Von Trapp (Wendy), sailor outfit 100.00
   10", #14030, Captain Von Trapp (Cissette), gray Tyrolean suit 125.00
   10", #13890, Maria at the Abbey (Cissette), navy dress, guitar 125.00
   10", #13870, Mother Superior (Cissette), Black and white nun habit 115.00
   10", #13880, Maria Travel Ensemble (Cissette), pleated skirt, bolero 125.00
   9", #14020, Friedrich von Trapp (Maggie), blue, gray sailor suit 100.00
   10", #14160, Louisa Von Trapp (Wendy), blue, gray pleated sailor 100.00
   10", #14090, Kurt Von Trapp (Wendy), sailor uniform 100.00
   10", #14170, Liesl Von Trapp (Cissette), blue, gray sailor outfit 100.00

SOUTH AMERICAN — 7" compo., 1938–1943 (Tiny Betty) 275.00
   9" compo., 1939–1941 (Little Betty) 300.00

SOUTHERN BELLE OR GIRL — 8" h.p., SLNW, 1953, white dress, straw hat w/pink silk roses . . . . .750.00 up
   8" h.p., #370, 1954 (Wendy Ann) . . . . .950.00 up
   8" h.p., #437, #410, 1956, pink or blue/white stripe gown (Wendy Ann) . . . . .1,000.00 up
   8" h.p., #385, 1963 only (Wendy Ann) 575.00
   12" h.p., 1963 only (Lissy) 1,500.00
   21" h.p./vinyl arms, #2155, 1965, blue gown with wide pleated hem (Jacqueline) 1,200.00

S

Southern Belle, 10", #1170, 1969 (Cissette). All original. Tagged: "Southern Belle."

Southern Belle, 8", 1953, SLNW, White long cotton gown with two rows of lace. Pink silk roses at waist and on straw hat. Tagged: "Alexander-Kins"

SOUTHERN BELLE OR GIRL, CONTINUED...

#2170, 1967, white gown with green ribbon trim 625.00
10" h.p., #1170, 1968, white gown with green ribbon through 3 rows of lace (Cissette) 450.00
1969, white gown with 4 rows of lace, pink sash (Cissette) 475.00
#1185, 1970, white gown with red ribbon sash (Cissette) 400.00
#1185 (#1184 in 1973) 1971–1973, white gown with green ribbon sash 350.00
10" (see My Doll House under Special Events/Exclusives)

SOUTHERN GIRL — 11–14" compo., 1940–1943 (Wendy Ann) 350.00–475.00
17–21" compo., 1940–1943 (Wendy Ann) 650.00–800.00

SOUTHERN SYMPOSIUM — (see M.A.D.C. under Special Events/Exclusives)

SPANISH — 7–8" compo., 1935–1939 (Tiny Betty) 275.00
9" compo., 1936–1940 (Litte Betty) 300.00

SPANISH BOY — 8" h.p., BK & BKW, #779, 1964–1968 (Wendy Ann) 375.00

SPANISH GIRL — 8" h.p., BKW, #795, #395, 1962–1965, three-tiered skirt (Wendy Ann) 150.00
8" h.p., BK, #795, 1965–1972, three-tiered skirt 100.00
8" straight leg, #0795, #595, 1973–1975, three-tiered skirt, marked "ALEX" 75.00
8" straight leg, #595, 1976–1982, three-tiered skirt, marked "Alexander" 65.00
8" straight leg, #595, 1983–1985, two-tiered skirt 60.00
8" straight leg, #541, 1986–1990, white with red polka dots (1986–1987 white face) 60.00
8" straight leg, #541, 1990–1992, all red tiered skirt 60.00
8" h.p., #110545, 1994–1995, red two-tiered polka dot gown 60.00
8" h.p., #24160, 1999, red rose and black gown 90.00

SPANISH MATADOR — 8", #530, 1992–1993 only (Wendy) 65.00

Shops and organizations are listed alphabetically.

ABC UNLIMITED PRODUCTIONS
  WENDY LEARNS HER ABC's — 8", 1993, wears blue jumper and beret, ABC blocks on skirt, wooden block stand, limit 3,200 . . . . .125.00

BELK & LEGGETT DEPARTMENT STORES
  MISS SCARLETT — 14", 1988 . . . . .150.00
  RACHEL/RACHAEL — 8", 1989, lavender gown 75.00
  NANCY JEAN — 8", 1990, yellow/brown outfit 75.00
  FANNIE ELIZABETH — 8", 1991, limited to 3,000, floral dress with pinafore 95.00
  ANNABELLE AT CHRISTMAS — 8", 1992, limited to 3,000, plaid dress, holds Christmas cards . . .125.00
  CAROLINE — 8", 1993, limit 3,600 . . . . .100.00
  HOLLY — 8", 1994, green eyes, freckles, wears red top with white skirt 95.00
  ELIZABETH BELK ANGEL — 8", #79648, 1996, red velvet 125.00

BLOOMINGDALE'S DEPARTMENT STORE
  10", 1997, coral and leopard Cissette with Bloomie's big brown bag 105.00

CELIA'S DOLLS
  DAVID, THE LITTLE RABBI — 8", 1991–1992, 3,600 made – 3 hair colors 75.00

CHILD AT HEART
  EASTER BUNNY — 8", 1991, limit: 3,000 (1,500 blondes, 750 brunettes, 750 redheads) 350.00
  MY LITTLE SWEETHEART — 8", 1992, limit: 4,500 (1,000 blondes, 1,000 brunettes w/blue eyes, 1,000 brunettes w/green eyes, 1,000 redheads w/green eyes, 500 blacks) 75.00
  TRICK AND TREAT — 8", 1993, sold in sets only
    (400 sets with red haired/green eyed "Trick" and black "Treat;"
    1,200 sets with red haired/green eyed "Trick" and brunette/brown eyed "Treat;"
    1,400 blonde/blue eyed "Trick" and red haired/brown eyed "Treat.") . . . . .190.00 set

CHRISTMAS SHOPPE
  BOY & GIRL, ALPINE — 8" twins, 1992, in Alpine Christmas outfits, limit 2,000 sets . . . . . .185.00 pair

COLLECTOR UNITED (C.U.)
C. U. GATHERING (GEORGIA)
  YUGOSLAVIA — 8", F.A.D., limit: 625 . . . . .100.00

Annabelle at Christmas, 8", 1992, Cissette head on 8" body. Made exclusively for Belk & Leggett Department stores. Limited to 3,000.

Elizabeth Belk Angel, 8", #79648, 1996, exclusive for Belk & Leggett Department stores (Wendy).

S

TIPPI BALLERINA — 8", 1988, limit: 800 ....425.00
MISS LEIGH — 8", 1989, limit: 800 ....125.00
SHEA ELF — 8", 1990, limit: 1,000 ....175.00
RINGMASTER — 8", 1991, limit: 800 ....125.00
FAITH — 8", 1992, limit: 800 ....250.00
HOPE — 8", 1993, limit: 900, blue dress (1910 style) 175.00
LOVE — 8", 1994, limit: 2,400, has gold necklace and pearls on cap 100.00
DIAN — 8", 1995, limit: 800, Back to the Fifties, ...150.00
C.U. VARSITY SWEATER — white sweater, 1995, special event souvenir 50.00
OLYMPIA — 8", 1996, ...150.00
OLYMPIC BAG — 1996, special Alexander event souvenir 50.00
C.U. SALUTES BROADWAY — 8", 1997, burgundy theatre outfit 175.00
BLACK FUR STOLE — 1997, special Alexander event souvenir 50.00
POLYNESIAN PRINCESS — 8", 1998, print skirt and top 175.00
GRASS SKIRT — 1998, special Alexander event souvenir 50.00
FORTUNE TELLER — 1999, 8", red print costume trimmed in gold 175.00
FORTUNE TELLER ACCESSORIES — scarfs and bangle bracelets, 1999, special event 50.00
FORTUNE TELLER — 1999, 21", red print costume trimmed in gold 600.00
CARNIVAL QUEEN — limited to 24, 1999, 16", pink or blue gown 300.00
MAJESTIC MIDWAY — 21", 1999, gold costume ....one of a kind

C.U. NASHVILLE WINTER WONDERLAND
NASHVILLE SKATER — 8", 1991, F.A.D., limit: 200 (Black Forest) 175.00
NASHVILLE SKIER — 8", 1992, F.A.D, limit: 200 (Tommy Tittlemouse) 100.00
FIRST COMES LOVE — 8", 1993, limit: 200, F.A.D. 250.00
CAPTAIN'S CRUISE — 1994, limit: 250, with trunk & wardrobe 200.00
NASHVILLE GOES COUNTRY — 8", 1995 ....150.00
NASHVILLE SUNNY — 8", 1996, yellow raincoat, hat 200.00
MISS TENNESSEE WALTZ — 8", long ballgown, coat 175.00
C.U. GOES TO CAMP — 8", 1998 ....150.00

C.U. GREENVILLE SHOW
BRIDE — 8", 1990, F.A.D. of Tommy Snooks, limit: 250 (Betsy Brooks) 125.00
WITCH/HALLOWEEN — 8", 1990, F.A.D., limit: 250 (Little Jumping Joan) 100.00
OKTOBERFEST — 8", 1992, F.A.D., limit: 200 ....125.00
C.U. COLUMBIA, S.C. CAMELOT — 8", 1991, F.A.D. (Maid Marian), limit: 400 ....125.00
C.U. JACKSONVILLE — 8" Greta, 1996, black doll, blue sundress 200.00

C.U. DOLL SHOP EXCLUSIVES
CAMEO LADY — 10", 1991, limit: 1,000, white dress, black trim 125.00
LE PETIT BOUDOIR — 10", 1993, F.A.D., limit: 700 ....100.00
AMERICA'S JUNIOR MISS — 8", 1994, white gown, medallion, limit: 1200 ....75.00
FITNESS — 8", 1995 ....75.00
JUDGE'S INTERVIEW — 8", 1996, limit: 500 ....75.00
TALENT — 8", 1996, gold tuxedo jacket, black shorts 75.00
EASTER OF YESTERYEAR — 8", 1995, comes with rabbit 75.00
SAILING WITH SALLY — 8", 1998, white dress, wooden boat 95.00
GARY GREEN — 8", 1998 ....75.00

DISNEY, WALT
DISNEY WORLD AUCTION — 21" one-of-kind dolls, therefore no prices shown.
SLEEPING BEAUTY — #1 in Series, 1989, 21", long blonde hair, in pink
with rhinestones and pearls
CHRISTINE (PHANTOM OF THE OPERA) — #2, 1990, blue/white outfit with white mask (Jacqueline)
QUEEN ISABELLA — #3, 1991, green/gold gown, long red hair (Jacqueline)
IT'S A GIRL — #4, 1992, comes with 8" baby in carriage (Cissy, Baby Genuis)
EMPEROR AND NIGHTINGALE — #4, 1992, 8" winged Wendy Ann. (23" Emperor bear by Gund)
WOMEN IN THE GARDEN — #5, 1993, four dolls (Cissette) dressed like 1867 Monet painting

S

CISSY BRIDE — 1923 and 8" FLOWER GIRL and RING BEARER. #5, 1993
ROMEO & JULIET — #6, 21" h.p., 1994, using 1950s bald nude "Maggie" dolls,
    rewigged, dressed in blue, burgundy and gold
SIR LANCELOT duLAC — #7, 1995, 1950s doll dressed in burgandy and gold
QUEEN GUINEVERE — #7, 1995, 1950s doll dressed in burgandy and gold
CHESS SET — 35 dolls from 8" to 21" on a satin chess board

ANNUAL SHOWCASE OF DOLLS

CINDERELLA — 10", 1989, #1, blue satin gown, limit: 250 . . . . .750.00
SNOW WHITE — 12", 1990, #2, limit: 750 (Nancy Drew) .175.00
ALICE IN WONDERLAND/WHITE RABBIT — 10", 1991, #3, limit: 750 .400.00
QUEEN OF HEARTS — 10", 1992, #4, limit: 500 . . . . .400.00
ALICE IN WONDERLAND/JABBERWOCKY — 11–12" (Lissy) 1993, limit: 500 .350.00
TWEEDLEDUM & TWEEDLEDEE — 8", 1994, #5, wear beany hats with propellers,
    names on collar, limit: 750 .325.00 pair
MORGAN LEFAY — 10", #797537, 1995, #6, limit: 500 .350.00
BOBBY (BOBBIE) SOXER — 8", 1990–1991 . . . . .200.00
MOUSEKETEER — 8", 1991 . . . . .200.00
ROLLER BLADES — 8", 1992, "Throughly Modern Wendy" 125.00
ROUND UP COWGIRL — 8", 1992, blue/white outfit 175.00
ANNETTE (FUNICELLO) — 14" porcelain portrait sculpted by Robert Tonner, 1993,
    limit: 400 . . . . .475.00
MONIQUE — 8", 1993, made for Disney, limit: 250, lavender with lace trim 600.00
SNOW WHITE — 10", 1993, Disney crest colors 200.00
BELLE — 8" h.p., gold gown, 1994 . . . . .125.00
CINDERELLA — 14", 1994, Disney catalog, has two outfits, limit: 900 . . . . .200.00
    14", 1995, different gown, no extra outfits 200.00
WENDY'S FAVORITE PASTIME — 8", 1994, comes with hula hoop 85.00
SLEEPING BEAUTY — 14", 1995, waist length hair,
    blue gown from movie and two other outfits 275.00
BLUE FAIRY TREE TOPPER — 10", #79545, 1995 catalog exclusive (Cissette) 150.00
SNOW WHITE — 14", 1995 . . . . .200.00
MARY POPPINS — 10", 1996, #79403 . . . . .125.00
ALICE — 14", 1996, limited to 1,500, catalog exclusive 175.00
KNAVE — 8", 1996, limited to 500, wears *2 of Spades* card .175.00
TOTO — 8", 1997, limited to 750, comes with wooden basket 175.00
GOLDILOCKS AND BABY BEAR — 8", 1998, purple print costume with Raikes Bear 250.00

DOLLS AND DUCKS

ICE PRINCESS — 8", 1999, silver gown and tiara 125.00

DOLL & TEDDY BEAR EXPO

MADAME (ALEXANDER) OR SHADOW OF MADAME — 8", 1994, in blue, limit: 500 first year 275.00
MADAME WITH LOVE — 8", #79536, 1995, has hat with 100 on top, limit: 750 . . . . .100.00
MAGGIE'S FIRST DOLL — 8", 1996, pink cotton dress, carries cloth Alice doll 225.00
MISS ELIZA DOOLITTLE — 21", 1996, white lace dress, one-of-a-kind auction piece
JOSEPHINE BAKER — 21", black Cissy, 1996, banana costume, one-of-a-kind auction piece

DOLL FINDERS

FANTASY — 8", 1990, limit: 350 . . . . .200.00

DOLLS 'N BEARLAND

PANDORA — 8", 1991, limit: 3,600 (950 brunette, 950 redheads, 1,700 blondes) 150.00

DOLLY DEARS

BO PEEP — 1987, holds staff, black sheep wears man's hat, white sheep wears woman's hat
    (Sheep made exclusively by Dakin) 225.00
SUSANNAH CLOGGER — 8", 1992, has freckles, limit: 400 (Maggie) 325.00
JACK BE NIMBLE — 8", 1993, F.A.D., limit: 288 . . . . .125.00
PRINCESS AND THE PEA — 8", 1993 limit: 1,000 . . . . .125.00

S

Elegant Doll Shop
Elegant Easter — 8", 1999, pink check with bunny 100.00
Heart of Dixie — 8", 1999, red and lace outfit 100.00

Enchanted Doll House
Rick-rack on pinafore — 8", 1980 limit: 3,000 . . . . .300.00
Eyelet pinafore — 8", 1981 limit: 3,423 . . . . .325.00
Blue or Pink Ballerina — 8", 1983–1985, F.A.D, blonde or brunette doll
   in trunk with extra clothes 175.00
Cinderella & Trunk — 14", has glass slipper, 1985 . . . . .275.00
25th Anniversary (The Enchanted Doll) — 10", 1988, long gown, limit: 5,000 . . . . .175.00
Ballerina — 8", 1989, blue tutu, limit: 360 . . . . .175.00
Vermont Maiden — 8", 1990–1992, official Vermont bicentennial doll, limit: 3,600
   (800 blondes, 2,800 brunettes) 100.00
Farmer's Daughter — 8", 1991, limit: 4,000 (1,000 blondes, 1,500 redheads, 1,500 brunettes) .100.00
Farmer's Daughter — 8", 1992, "Goes To Town" (cape and basket added), limit: 1,600 . . . .125.00

FAO Schwarz
Pussy Cat — 18", 1987, pale blue dress and bonnet 150.00
Brooke — 14", 1988, blonde or brunette (Mary Ann) with Steiff Bear 125.00
David and Diana — 8", 1989, in red, white, and demin, with wooden wagon . . . . .175.00 set
Samantha — 14", 1989, white with black dots (Mary Ann) 150.00
Me & My Scassi — 21", 1990, dressed in all red Arnold Scassi original (Cissy) 375.00
Sailor — 8", 1991 . . . . .125.00
Carnavale Doll — 14", 1991–1992 (Samatha) 185.00
Beddy-Bye Brooke — 14", 1991–1992 (Mary Ann) 125.00
   Beddy-Bye Brenda (Brooke's sister) — 8", 1992, sold only as set with 14" doll . . . . . .225.00 set
Wendy Shops FAO — 8", 1993, red/white outfit, carries FAO Schwarz shopping bag 125.00
My Secret Garden — 8", trunk with wardrobe 1994 . . . . .350.00
Little Huggums — 12", red dress, bib & headband, has FAO logo horse 1994 . . . . .65.00
Little Women — 8", 1994, dressed in outfits from movie, limit: 500 sets (5 dolls) and
   700 of each girl . . . . .125.00each . . . . .750.00 set
Princess trunk set — 8", #79526, 1995 . . . . .250.00
Fun with Dick & Jane — 8", #70509, 1995, 1,200 pieces . . . . .175.00 set
Lucy Ricardo — 8", limited to 1,200 . . . . .200.00
I Love Lucy — 8" Fred, Ethel, Lucy, and Ricky, sold as set only, limit: 1,200 . . . . .700.00 set
The Little Rascals — 8" Alfalfa, Darla, Spanky, Buckwheat,
   and dog Petey, 1996, ...2,000 sets 525.00
Singing in the Rain — 8" Gene Kelly, Debbie Reynolds with lamppost, 1996, 1952 film . . .300.00
I Dream of Jeannie — 8", harem outfit, 8", military uniform 275.00
Lucy and Ethel — 8", 1997, candy factory episode 190.00
The Honeymooners — 8", 1997, Ralph, Alice, Norton, Trixie, 2,000 sets 425.00
Grease — 1998, 10" 175.00
Fay Wray with Steiff King Kong — 1998 . . . . .500.00

First Modern Doll Club (N.Y. Doll club)
Autumn in N.Y. — 10", 1991, F.A.D., red skirt, fur trim cape/hat/muff/skates, limit: 260 . . . . .175.00

Home Shopping Network
Blue Angel — 8", 1997, #19972, dark blue and gold dress and halo,
   resin wings, limit: 3000 . . . . .200.00

Horchow
Pamela Plays Dress Up — 12", 1993, in trunk with wardrobe, limit: 1,250 (Lissy) 325.00
Pamela Trousseau — 12", 1994, trunk and trousseau. Limit 265 . . . . .325.00
   14" trunk set, 1995 . . . . .250.00
Mary Ann Dances for Grandma Trunk Set — 14", 1996 . . . . .300.00

I. Magnin
Cheerleader — 8", 1990, F.A.D., "5" on sweater 100.00
Miss Magnin — 10", 1991–1993, limit: 2,500 (Cissette) 150.00

I. MAGNIN

LITTLE HUGGUMS — 12" with cradle 1992 . . . . .125.00
LITTLE MISS MAGNIN — 8", 1992, with tea set and teddy bear, limit: 3,600 . . . . .175.00
BON VOYAGE MISS MAGNIN — 10", 1993, navy/white gloves,
   has steamer trunk, limit: 2,500 . . . . .195.00
BON VOYAGE LITTLE MISS MAGNIN — 8", sailor dress, carries teddy bear/suitcase,
   limit: 3,500, 1993 . . . . .150.00
LITTLE MISS MAGNIN SUPPORTS THE ARTS — 8", 1994, pink painter smock,
   wears red ribbon for AIDS Awareness 175.00

IMAGINARIUM SHOP (I. MAGNINS)

LITTLE HUGGUMS 12", 1991, special outfits, bald or wigged, 2 wig colors 50.00

JACOBSONS

WENDY STARTS HER COLLECTION — 1994, has bear, limit: 2,400 . . . . .150.00
LITTLE HUGGUMS — 1995 . . . . .65.00

JEAN'S DOLL SHOP

SUELLEN — 12", 1992 F.A.D. 135.00
WENDY WALKS HER DOG — 8", #79549, 1995, 500 pieces 95.00

LILLIAN VERNON

CHRISTMAS DOLL — 8", #79630, 1996, green and gold holly print dress 100.00

LORD & TAYLOR

VICTORIA — 14", 1989 . . . . .85.00

MADAME ALEXANDER DOLL CLUB (M.A.D.C.) CONVENTION DOLLS

FAIRY GODMOTHER OUTFIT — 1983, for 8" non-Alexander designed by Judy LaManna 350.00
BALLERINA — 8", 1984, F.A.D. limit: 360 . . . . .250.00
HAPPY BIRTHDAY — 8", 1985, F.A.D. limit: 450 . . . . .325.00
SCARLETT — 8", 1986, F.A.D., red instead of green ribbon, limit: 625 . . . . .250.00
COWBOY — 8", 1987, limit: 720 . . . . .450.00
FLAPPER — 10", 1988, F.A.D., black outfit instead of red, limit: 720 . . . . .225.00
BRIAR ROSE — 8", 1989, uses Cissette head, limit: 804 . . . . .300.00
RIVERBOAT QUEEN (LENA) — 8", 1990, limit: 025 . . . . .300.00
QUEEN CHARLOTTE — 10", 1991, blue/gold outfit, limit: under 900 . . . . .350.00
PROM QUEEN (MEMORIES) — 8", 1992, limit: 1,100 . . . . .225.00
DRUCILLA — 14" 1992, limit: 268 . . . . .200.00
DIAMOND LIL (DAYS GONE BY) — 10", 1993, black gown, limit: 876 . . . . .300.00
ANASTASIA — 14" 1993, F.A.D., available at convention, limit: 489 . . . . .225.00
NAVAJO WOMEN — 8", 1994, comes with rug, sheep, and Hopi Kachina, limit: 835 . . . . . . .350.00
FLOWERGIRL — 8", companion to 1995 souvenir doll, could be purchased separately 125.00
FOLSOM, FRANCES — 10", 1995 convention doll, #79517 (married Grover Cleveland) 275.00
SHOWGIRL — 10", 1996 convention doll, pink, blue, green, lavender, white feathers 300.00
   10", 1996 convention, black feather, 20 pieces 500.00
A LITTLE BIT OF COUNTRY — 8", 1997, #79080, with guitar 250.00
ROSE FESTIVAL QUEEN — 8", #79450, 1998, white gown, cape with roses 275.00
MARGARET O'BRIEN — 1998 Convention Companion doll, 8", #79590 . . . . .175.00
ORANGE BLOSSOM — 10", 1999, peach long dress and gold straw hat 250.00
ELECTRA — 8", 1999, Convention Companion doll, silver costume 80.00

M.A.D.C. DOLLS, EXCLUSIVES (AVAILABLE TO CLUB MEMBERS ONLY)

WENDY — 8", 1989, in pink and blue, limit: 4,878 . . . . .175.00
POLLY PIGTAILS — 8", 1990 (Maggie Mixup) limit: 4,896 . . . . .150.00
MISS LIBERTY — 10", 1991–1992, red/white/blue gown (Cissette) 125.00
LITTLE MISS GODEY — 8", 1992–1993 . . . . .150.00
WENDY'S BEST FRIEND MAGGIE — 8", 1994 . . . . .100.00
WENDY LOVES BEING BEST FRIENDS — 8", name embroidered on apron, 1994 . . . . .100.00
WENDY LOVES THE DIONNES — 8", one-of-kind set of 5 dolls
   made for 1994 convention . . . . .Not Available
ULTIMATE CISSY — 21", one-of-kind for 1996 convention . . . . .Not Available
WENDY JOINS M.A.D.C. — 8", #79552, 1995 . . . . .225.00
WENDY HONORS MARGARET WINSON — 8", 1996 postmistress outfit, honoring
   first M.A.D.C. president 100.00

S

FROM THE MADAME'S SKETCHBOOK — 8", 1997, replica of 1930s Tiny Betty 75.00
SKATE WITH WENDY — 8", 1998, plaid skating outfit, silver key 80.00
ELECTRO — 8", 1999, (Maggie) silver space costume, boy 80.00

M.A.D.C. SYMPOSIUM/PREMIERE

PRE-DOLL SPECIALS (M.A.D.C. SYMPOSIUM)

DISNEYWORLD — 1984–1985 (1984 paper doll) 60.00
WENDY GOES TO DISNEYWORLD — #1 Sunshine Symposium, 1986, navy dress with polka dots,
    Mickey Mouse hat, pennant (costume by Dorothy Starling), limit: 100 . . . . .125.00

SNOWFLAKE SYMPOSIUM

1st Illinois, 1986, tagged orange taffeta/lace dress, metal pail and orange, limit: 200 . . .85.00
2nd Illinois, 1987, tagged, little girl cotton print dress (costume by Mary Voigt) 85.00
3rd Illinois, 1988, tagged, gold/white print dress, gold bodice (created by Pamela Martenec)85.00
4th Illinois, 1989, tagged, red velvet ice skating costume (created by Joan Dixon) 95.00
5th Illinois, 1990, bride by Linda Bridal Shop (also Michelau Scarlett could be purchased) .95.00
SCARLETT — 8", 1990, #6, F.A.D. (white medallion – Snowflake Symposium; red medallion –
    Premier Southern Symposium) limit: 800 . . . . .175.00
(Medallions: Midwest – rose; Southwest – peach; Southeast – blue; Northeast – lavender; West Coast – yellow; Northwest – green)
SPRINGTIME — 8", 1991, #7, floral dress, scalloped pinafore, straw hat, limit: 1,600 . . . . . .250.00
WINTERTIME — 8", 1992, #8, all white, fur trim and hat (six locations), limit: 1,650 . . . . . . .250.00
HOMECOMING — 8", 1993, #9 car coat with color trim (8 different colors – one for each location),
    limit: 2,000 . . . . .225.00
SETTING SAIL FOR SUMMER — 8" 1994, #10 (eight locations), limit: 1,800 . . . . .150.00
SNOWFLAKE — 8", #79404, 1995 (6 locations) gold skater, limit: 1,200 . . . . .175.00
WENDY STARTS HER TRAVELS — 8", 1996 (3 locations), trunk set, different color checked coat
    each location 250.00
BOBBY TAKES A PICTURE — 8", 1996, 215 pieces, California companion doll 150.00
CHESHIRE CAT — 8", 1996, 215 pieces, Texas companion doll 200.00
WENDY TOURS THE FACTORY — 8", 1996, New Jersey companion doll 150.00
WENDY'S TEA PARTY — 8", 1997 (4 locations), pink organie dress, tea set 175.00
BOO — 8", 1996, 150 pieces, ghost costume over Mother's Day doll 125.00
DIAMOND PIXIE — 8", 1998 (3 locations), red Pixie costume 195.00
STARLETT GLAMOUR — 10", 1999, black evening gown 225.00

M.A.D.C. FRIENDSHIP LUNCHEON

FRIENDS AROUND THE COUNTRY — print dress and pinafore outfit 50.00

MADAME ALEXANDER DOLL COMPANY

MELODY & FRIENDS — 25", 1992, limit: 1,000, designed and made by Hilegard Gunzel,
    first anniversary dolls . . . . .700.00 up set
COURTNEY & FRIENDS — 25" & 8" boy and girl, 1993,
    second anniverary, limit: 1,200, by Gunzel . . . . 725.00 up set
RUMPELSTILTSKIN & MILLER'S DAUGHTER — 8" & 14", #1569, 1992 only, limit: 3,000 . . . . 300.00
SPECIAL EVENT DOLL — 8", 1994, organza and lace in pink with special event banner,
    ribbon across body, front of hair pulled back in curls 65.00
WENDY MAKES IT SPECIAL — 8", 1998, #31050, pink and white dress, hat box 100.00
WENDY SALUTES THE OLYMPICS — 8", #86005, 1996, Olympic medal 150.00
MAGGIE MIXUP — 8", 1998, #31000, Post Office commemorative, blue gingham 75.00
75TH ANNIVERSARY WENDY — 8", #22420, 1998, pink outfit 110.00
WENDY'S SPECIAL CHEER — 8", #16510, cheerleader, 1999 . . . . .75.00
GEORGE AND MARTHA WASHINGTON — 8", 1999, limited . . . . .200.00 set
MARY MCFADDEN CISSY — 21", 1999, black and gold gown .one of a kind
ISAAC MIZRAHI CISSY — 21", 1999, gray skirt, red sweaters . . . . .one of a kind
CARMEN MARC VALVO CISSY — 21", 1999, long evening gown . . . . .one of a kind
NICOLE MILLER — 21", 1999, dress and fur coat . . . . .one of a kind
DIANE VON FURSTENBERG CISSY — 21", 1999, black dress, fur coat . . . . .one of a kind
YEOHLEE CISSY — 21", 1999, black skirt, long black coat . . . . .one of a kind
BETSY JOHNSON CISSY — 21", 1999, black short dress trimmed in pink . . . . .one of a kind
SCAASI CISSY — 21", 1999, white lace gown, red coat with feather . . . . .one of a kind

The 1999 designer Cissys on page 80 plus the original designer Cissys below are to be auctioned for "Fashion Targets Breast Cancer." The Cissys below were made in limited editions for 1999.

Wicked Witch, 8", 1994 (Maggie). Wizard of Oz Series.

JESSICA MCCLINTOCK CISSY — 21", 1999, #22780,
   long gold ball gown 450.00
FERNANDO SANCHEZ CISSY — 21", 1999, #22720,
   white long gown 450.00
JOSIE NATORI CISSY — 21", 1999, #22730 . . . . .450.00
ANNA SUI CISSY — 21", 1999, #22590, has braids,
   brown dress, coat 450.00
LINDA ALLARD FOR ELLEN TRACY CISSY — 21", 1999,
   brown skirt, black long coat 450.00
DANA BUCHMAN CISSY — 21", 1999, green dress, coat . . .450.00
DONNA KARAN CISSY — 21", 1999, black long dress 450.00
JAMES PURCELL CISSY — 21", 1999, white long gown,
   with black circles 450.00
MADAME ALEXANDER CELEBRATES AMERICAN DESIGN CISSY — 21",
   1999, #22560 . . . . .450.00
BADGLEY MISCHKA CISSY — 21", 1999, #22740,
   long evening gown 450.00
MARC BOUWER CISSY — 21", 1999, #26125, African American doll, long gown 450.00
CAROLINA HERRERA CISSY — 21", 1999, #26121, red and white ball gown 450.00
"AN AMERICAN LEGEND" BOOK AND DOLL in display box 250.00

MID-YEAR SPECIALS FOR MADAME ALEXANDER DOLL COMPANY

WELCOME HOME — 8", 1991, black or white, boy or girl, Desert Storm Soldier 50.00
WENDY LOVES BEING LOVED — 8", 1992, doll and wardrobe 150.00
QUEEN ELIZABETH II — 8", 1992, 40th anniversary of coronation 150.00
CHRISTOPHER COLUMBUS — 8", 1992, #328, burgundy and brown costume 125.00
QUEEN ISABELLA — 8", 1992, #329, green velvet and gold gown 125.00
SANTA OR MRS. CLAUS — 8", 1993 . . . . .100.00 each
SCARLETT O'HARA — 8", 1993, yellow dress, straw hat 150.00
WENDY ANN — 8", 1995, 100th anniversary, pink coat and hat 125.00
SIR LANCELOT DULAC — 8", 1995, burgundy and gold knight's costume 125.00
QUEEN GUINEVERE — 8", 1995, burgundy and gold gown 125.00
WIZARD OF OZ — 8", 1994 . . . . 125.00
DOROTHY — 8", 1994, emerald green checked dress 125.00
WICKED WITCH — 8", 1994, green face, black costume 175.00

MARSHALL FIELDS
   AVRIL, JANE — 10", 1989, red/black can-can outfit (tribute to T. Lautrec) (Cissette) 150.00
   MADAME BUTTERFLY — 10", 1990 . . . . .150.00
METROPLEX DOLL CLUB
   SPRING BREAK — 8", 1992, 2-piece halter/wrap skirt outfit, limit: 400, beach bag 250.00
MEYERS 80TH YEAR
   8", "Special Event" doll with banner 1994 . . . . .75.00
MY DOLL HOUSE
   SOUTHERN BELLE — 10", 1989, F.A.D., all pink gown with parasol and picture hat,
      limit: 2,300 . . . . .150.00
   QUEEN ELIZABETH I — 10", 1990, limit: 2,400 . . . . .150.00
   EMPRESS ELIZABETH OF AUSTRIA — 10", 1991, white/gold trim, limit: 3,600 (Cissette) 150.00
NEIMAN-MARCUS
   DOLL WITH FOUR OUTFITS IN TRUNK — 8", 1990, called "party trunk," limit: 1,044 . . . . .250.00

S

CAROLINE LOVES STORYLAND — 8", 1993, trunk and wardrobe 275.00
CAROLINE'S ADVENTURES — 8", 1994, trunk and costumes for USA, China, Germany, Kenya (Maggie) . . .250.00
ANNE SERIES — 8", 1994, trunk set, character from Lucy M. Montgomery books 275.00

NEW ENGLAND COLLECTOR SOCIETY
NOEL — 12", 1989–1991, porcelain Christmas doll, limit: 5,000 . . . . .250.00
JOY — 12", 1991, porcelain Christmas doll, limit: 5,000 .225.00

NEW YORK DOLL CLUB
AUTUMN IN NEW YORK — 10" F.A.D., limit: 260 . . . . .175.00

QVC
SUMMER CHERRY PICKING — 8", #79760, 1998 (Wendy), limited to 500 . . . . .150.00
BETSY ROSS — 8", #79990, 1998 (Wendy), limited to 500 .100.00
PILGRIM GIRL — 8", #79980, 1998 (Wendy), limited to 500 . . . . .100.00
HOME FOR THE HOLIDAYS — 10", #79800, 1998 (Cissette), limited to 400 . . . . .150.00
A ROSE FOR YOU — 8", 1999, (Wendy) 95.00
LAVENDER ROSE — 10", 1999, lavender ball gown 150.00
POLLYANNA — 8", 1999, (Maggie) 95.00
BLOSSOM — 8", 1999, pink print dress (Wendy) 95.00
LITTLE BO PEEP — 100.00
INVESTIGATOR WENDY — 8", 1999 (checked coat and hat) 100.00

SAKS FIFTH AVENUE
CHRISTMAS CAROL — 8", 1993 . . . . .125.00
JOY OF CHRISTMAS — 1994, 2nd in series 125.00

SEARS-ROEBUCK
LITTLE WOMEN — 1989–1990, set of six 12" dolls
(Nancy Drew) . . . . .500.00 set

SHIRLEY'S DOLL HOUSE
ANGEL FACE — 8", 1990 (Maggie Mixup) limit: 3,500 . . . . .125.00
WINTER SPORTS — 8", 1991, FAD (Tommy Snooks) limit: 975 .75.00
WENDY VISITS WORLD FAIR — 1993, 100th anniversary Chicago
World's Fair, limit: 3,600 .95.00

Investigator Wendy, 8", 1999. An exclusive for QVC (Wendy). Comes with magnifying glass.

WINTER ANGEL — 1993, has cape with hood, wings, and
holds golden horn, exclusive: 1,000 . . . . .125.00
MAYPOLE DANCE — 8", 1994, shop's 20th anniversary doll,
pink organdy dress and blue pinafore,
limit: 3,000 (Wendy Ann) .75.00
GRANDMA'S DARLING — 8", 1996, #79617, yellow dress,
white blanket 75.00

SHRINER'S 1ST LADIES LUNCHEON
8" boy, 1993, wears fez, jeans, shirt,
vest/Texas star on back, limit: 1,800 . . . . .450.00 up

SPIEGEL'S
BETH — 10", 1990, 125th anniversary special,
1860s women 125.00
CHRISTMAS TREE TOPPER (ALSO CALLED MERRY ANGEL) —
8", 1991 . . . . .150.00
JOY NOEL — 8", 1992, tree topper angel, white satin/net with
gold dots, gold lace, halo & skirt, limit: 3,000 . . . . . .125.00
MARDI GRAS — 10", 1992, elaborate costume of . . . .
purple/gold/royal blue, limit: 3,000 . . . . .150.00

U.F.D.C. – UNITED FEDERATION OF DOLL CLUBS
SAILOR BOY — 8", limit: 260 . . . . .750.00
MISS UNITY — 10", 1991, limit: 310 . . . . .400.00
LITTLE EMPEROR — 8", 1992, limit: 400 . . . . .500.00

TURN OF THE CENTURY BATHING BEAUTY — 10", 1992, U.F.D.C.
Region Nine Conference,F.A.D. (Gibson Girl), old-fashion
bathing suit, beach bag, and umbrella, limit: 300 ....275.00
COLUMBIAN 1893 SAILOR — 12", 1993 (Lissy) 250.00
GABRIELLE — 10", 1998 (Cissette), limited: 400, black suit, dressmaker's stand 325.00
ONE ENCHANTED EVENING — 16", 1999, #80260, limited to 300

―――――――――― END OF SPECIAL EVENTS/EXCLUSIVES ――――――――――

SPECIAL GIRL — 23–24" cloth/compo., 1942–1946 ....500.00
SPIEGEL'S — (see Spiegel's under Special Events/Exclusives)
SPRING — 14", 1993, Changing Seasons, doll and four outfits 125.00
SPRINGTIME — 8" (see M.A.D.C. under Special Events/Exclusives)
SPRING BREAK — (see Metroplex Doll Club under Special Events/Exclusives)
STARLIGHT ANGEL — 10", #10790, 1999, (Cissette) star-accented gown 110.00
STEPMOTHER — 8", 1997, #13820, velvet cape, satin dress 80.00
STICK PIGGY — 12", 1997, #10030, sailor outfit 85.00
STILTS — 8", #320, 1992–1993 only, clown on stilts 85.00
STRAW PIGGY — 12", 1997, #10020, plaid pants, straw hat 85.00
STORY PRINCESS — 15–18" h.p., 1954–1956 (Margaret, Cissy, Binnie) 550.00–850.00
    8" h.p., #892, 1956 only (Wendy Ann) ....1,300.00 up
STUFFY (BOY) — h.p., 1952–1953 (Margaret) 875.00
SUELLEN — 14–17" compo., 1937–1938 (Wendy Ann) ....975.00 up
    12", 1990 only, yellow multi-tiered skirt, Scarlett Series (Nancy Drew) 85.00
    8" pink bodice, floral skirt, apron, #160645, 1994–1995 ....85.00
    Special for Jean's Doll Shop (see Special Events/Exclusives) 125.00
SUELLEN O'HARA — 8", #15200, 1999 ....80.00
SUGAR AND SPICE — 8", #13530, 1998–1999, pink and white lace dress 90.00
SUGAR DARLIN' — 14–18" cloth/vinyl, 1964 only 75.00–125.00
    24", 1964 only 150.00
    Lively, 14", 18", 24", 1964 only, knob makes head & limbs move 125.00–200.00
SUGAR PLUM FAIRIE — 10", #1147, 1992–1993 only, Portrette, lavender ballerina 100.00
SUGAR PLUM FAIRY— 8" (Wendy), 1999, #12640, pink satin and tulle 76.00
SUGAR TEARS — 12" vinyl baby, 1964 only (Honeybea) 110.00
SULKY SUE — 8", #445, 1988–1990, marked "Alexander" (Wendy Ann) 75.00
SUMMER — 14", 1993, Changing Seasons, doll and four outfits 135.00
SUNBEAM — 11", 16", 19", 1951 only, newborn infant, clean and in fair condition ...75.00–150.00
    16", 20", 24" cloth/vinyl, 1950, Divine-a-lite series (reg #573, 313), scowling expression 125.00
SUNBONNET SUE — 9" compo., 1937–1940 (Little Betty) 300.00
SUNFLOWER CLOWN — 40" all cloth, 1951 only, flower eyes 850.00up
SUNNY — 8" (see C.U. under Special Events/Exclusives)
SUSANNAH CLOGGER — 8" (see Dolly Dears under Special Events/Exclusives)
SUSIE Q — Cloth, 1940–1942 ....650.00
    8", #14590, 1995, Toy Shelf Series, has yarn braids and pink polka dot dress
        with green jacket 75.00
SUZY — 12" plastic/vinyl, 1970 only (Janie) 325.00
SWAN PRINCESS — 10", #14106, 1995 only, Fairy Tales Series 85.00
SWAN LAKE — 16", #22040, 1998, Odette in white tutu 195.00
SWEDEN (SWEDISH) — 8 h.p., BKW, #392, #792, 1961–1965 (Wendy Ann) 125.00

  8" h.p., BK, #792, 1965–1972 . . . . .100.00
  8" straight leg, #0792, #592, 1973–1975, marked "Alex" 75.00
  8" straight leg, #592, #539, #521, 1976–1989, marked "Alexander" 65.00
  8", 1986 . . . . .55.00
  8", #580, reintroduced 1991 only 55.00
  BKW with Maggie smile face 185.00
SWEDISH — 7" compo., 1936–1940 (Tiny Betty) 285.00
  9" compo., 1937–1941 (Little Betty) 300.00
SWEET BABY — 18½"–20" cloth/latex, 1948 only 50.00–100.00
SWEET BABY — 14", 1983–1984 (Sweet Tears) 75.00
  14", reissued 1987, 1987–1993 (1991 has no bottle) (Sweet Tears) 85.00
  14", 1990–1992 only (1991 has bottle), in carrycase 125.00
  14", reintroduced 1993 only, pink stripe jumper or dress 85.00
SWEET SIXTEEN — 14", #1554, 1991–1992 only, Classic Series (Louisa) 125.00
  10", #21060, 1997, pink silk dress, lace stole 95.00
SWEET TEARS — 9" vinyl, 1965–1974 . . . . .85.00
  9" with layette in box 1965–1973 . . . . .175.00
  14", 1967–1974, in trunk/trousseau 200.00
  14", 1965–1974, in window box 175.00
  14", 1979, with layette 125.00
  14", 1965–1982 . . . . .75.00
  16", 1965–1971 . . . . .75.00
SWEET VIOLET — 18" h.p., 1951–1954 (Cissy) . . . . .875.00 up
SWEETIE BABY — 22", 1962 only 125.00
SWEETIE WALKER — 23", 1962 only . . . . .275.00 up
SWISS — 7" compo., 1936 (Tiny Betty) 265.00

  9" compo., 1935–1938 (Little Betty) 275.00
  10" h.p., 1962–1963 (Cissette) 825.00
SWITZERLAND — 8" h.p., BKW, #394, #794,
    1961–1965 .125.00
  8" h.p., BK, #794, 1965–1972 . . . . .100.00
  8" h.p., straight leg, #0794, #594, 1973–1975,
    marked "Alex" 75.00
  8" h.p., straight leg, #594, #540, #518,
    1976–1989, marked "Alexander" . . .65.00
  8", #546, 1986 . . . . .60.00
  #518, 1988–1990, costume change 60.00
  8" BKW, Maggie smile face 175.00
SYMPOSIUM (see M.A.D.C. under Special
    Events/Exclusives)

Swedish, 8", #792, 1965 (Wendy).
BKW. Mint with original wrist tag.

••••••••••••••••••• PLEASE READ "WHAT IS A PRICE GUIDE?" FOR ADDITIONAL INFORMATION ••••••••••••••••••

TAFT, HELEN — 1988, 5th set Presidents' Ladies/First Ladies Series (Louisa) 125.00
TARA — #14990, 1998, 2 sided home of scarlet 200.00
TAURUS — 8", #21340,1998 – brown and white bull costume 90.00
TEA ROSE CISSETTE — 10", #22370 – 1998, floral silk cocktail dress 165.00
TEAM CANADA — 8", #24130, 1998–1999, hockey skater 80.00
TEENY TWINKLE — 1946 only, cloth with flirty eyes 525.00
TENNIS — 8" h.p., BKW, #415, #632 (Wendy Ann) 450.00
TENNIS BOY— 8", #16331, 1997 ....60.00
TENNIS GIRL — 8", #16320, 1997 ....60.00
TEXAS — 8", #313, 1991 only, Americana 85.00

Sweet Violet, 18", 1954, hard plastic, fully jointed walker (Cissy).

Thailand, 8", #767, 1967 (Wendy). Bend knees with very dark skin.

TEXAS SHRINER — (see Shriner's under Special Events/Exclusives)
THAILAND — 8" h.p., BK, #767, 1966–1972 (Wendy) 100.00
   8" straight leg, #0767, #567, 1973–1975, marked "Alex" 75.00
   8" straight leg, #567, 1976–1989, marked "Alexander" 65.00
THANK YOU — 8", #21110, 1997 – 1998, comes with a thank-you card 60.00
THERE WAS A LITTLE GIRL — 14", #24611, 1995, Nursery Rhyme Series (Mary Ann) 90.00
"THERE'S NO PLACE LIKE HOME" DOLLHOUSE — trunk set, #13260, 1997–1999 ....150.00
THINKING OF YOU — 8", #21500, 1998–1999, print dress, straw hat 80.00
THOMAS, MARLO — 17" plastic/vinyl, 1967 only (Polly) ....600.00 up
THREE LITTLE PIGS SET — 12", #10000, brick, straw, and stick Piggy 285.00
THREE LITTLE PIGS & WOLF — compo., 1938–1939, must be mint ....675.00 up each
THREE WISE MEN SET — 8", #19480, 1997–1999, Nativity set 340.00
THUMBELINA & HER LADY — 8" & 21" porcelain, 1992–1993, limit: 2,500 sets 500.00
TIERNEY, GENE — 14–17" compo., 1945, must be mint (Wendy Ann) 3,300.00
TIBET — 8" h.p., #534, 1993 only 75.00
TIGER LILY — 8", #469, 1992–1993 only, Storybook Series (Peter Pan) (Wendy Ann) 95.00
TIMMY TODDLER 23" plastic/vinyl, 1960–1961 ...150.00
   30", 1960 only 250.00
TINKERBELL — 11" h.p., #1110, 1969 only, Peter Pan Series (Cissette) ....475.00 up
   8" h.p., #140467 in 1991–1993; Storyland Series in 1994, has magic wand and wings, #13960 in 1998–1999 ....75.00
   14", #87009, 1996 (Mary Ann) 105.00
TINKLES — 8", #10400, 1995, Christmas Series 55.00
TIN MAN — 8", #13210, 1998–1999, Wizard of Oz Series 70.00
TIN WOODSMAN — 8", #432 in 1993, #140432 in 1994–1995 ....70.00
TINY BETTY — 7" compo., 1935–1942 ....275.00
TINY TIM — 7" compo., 1934–1937 (Tiny Betty) 325.00
   14" compo., 1938–1940 (Wendy Ann) 625.00
   Cloth, early 1930s 700.00
   8", #18001, 1996, Dickens (Wendy Ann) 65.00
TIPPI BALLERINA — 8" (see Collectors United under Special Events/Exclusives)
TIPPY TOE — 16" cloth, 1940s 600.00
TOM SAWYER — 8" h.p., #491, 1989–1990, Storybook Series (Maggie Mixup) 90.00
TOMMY — 12" h.p., 1962 only (Lissy) 1,000.00
TOMMY BANGS — h.p., 1952 only, Little Men Series (Maggie, Margaret) 875.00
TOMMY SNOOKS — 8", #447, 1988–1991, Storybook Series 75.00
TOMMY TITTLEMOUSE — 8", #444, 1988–1991, Storybook Series (Maggie) 70.00
TOOTH FAIRY — 10" Portrette, 1994 only 90.00

8", #10389–10391, 1995 only, Special Occasion Series, three hair colors 65.00
8", #21550, 1999, pink sparkling outfit, satin pillow 80.00
TONY SARG MARIONETTES see Marionettes
TOPSY-TURVY — compo. with Tiny Betty heads, 1935 only 275.00
   With Dionne Quint head, 1936 only 350.00
    CINDERELLA — #14587, 1995 only, two head, one side gown; other side dress with apron 125.00
    RED RIDING HOOD — 8", #14555 (3 way) Red Riding Hood, Grandma, Wolf 125.00
    WICKED STEPMOTHER — 8", #14640, 1996, evil witch, stepmother .160.00
TOULOUSE-LAUTREC — 21", #2250, 1986–1987 only, black/pink outfit 325.00
TOY SOLDIER — 8", #481, 1993, #140481, 1994, #13210 – 1998, white face, red dots on cheeks 75.00
TRAIN JOURNEY — 8", h.p., #486, 1955, white wool jacket, hat, red plaid dress 450.00
TRAPEZE ARTIST — 10", #1133, 1990–1991, Portrette (Cissette) 100.00
TREE TOPPER — 8" (½ doll only), #850, 1992 only, red/gold dress 100.00
   8" (½ doll only), #852, 1992–1994, ANGEL LACE with multi-tiered ivory lace skirt (Wendy) 110.00
   8" (½ doll only), #853, 1993–1994, red velvet/gold & green (Wendy) 100.00
   10" (½ doll only), #854, 1993–1994; #54854–1995, pink Victorian (Cissette) 125.00
   8" (½ doll only), #540855, 1994; #540855–1995, all antique white (Wendy) 110.00
   8", #84857, 1995–1996, YULETIDE ANGEL dressed in red and gold (Wendy), #19600, 1997 . . . . .85.00
   8", #84859, 1995–1996, CHRISTMAS ANGEL dressed in white and gold (Wendy) 85.00
   10", #54860, GLORIOUS ANGEL dressed in red and white, gold crown, #19590, 1997 – 1998 (Cissette) . .110.00
   10", #19610, 1997 – 1998, HEAVENLY ANGEL, gold and ivory costume (Wendy) 110.00
   10", GLISTENING ANGEL, 1998–1999, #19700 (Wendy), silver brocade .125.00
   10", WINTER LIGHTS; #20000, 1999, AC illuminated 135.00
TREENA BALLERINA — 15" h.p., 1952 only, must be near mint (Margaret) . . . . .700.00 up
   18–21", 1952 only 650.00–875.00
TRICK AND TREAT — (see Child at Heart under Special Events/Exclusives)
TRUMAN, BESS — 14", 1989–1990, 6th set First Ladies/Presidents' Ladies Series (Mary Ann) 125.00
TUNISIA — 8", #514, 1989 only, marked "Alexander" (Wendy) 70.00
TURKEY — 8" h.p., BK, #787, 1968–1972 (Wendy) 125.00
   8" straight leg, #0787, #587, 1973–1975, marked "Alex" 75.00
   8" straight leg, #587, 1976–1986, marked "Alexander" 65.00
TWEEDLEDUM & TWEEDLEDEE — 14" cloth, 1930–1931 . . . . .725.00 each
   8" h.p., #13080, 1998–1999, checked pants, red jacket, propeller caps .165.00
   (see Disney under Special Events/Exclusives)
TWILIGHT ANGEL — 8", #10780, (Wendy) 1999, white organza gown 105.00
TWINKLE, TWINKLE LITTLE STAR — 8", #11630, 1997 . . . . .65.00
20S BRIDE — #14103, 1995, Nostalgia Series 100.00
20S TRAVELER — 10", #1139, 1991–1992 only, Portrette, M.A. signature logo on box (Cissette) 125.00
25TH ANNIVERSARY — 1982 (see Enchanted Doll House Special Events/Exclusives)
TYLER, JULIA — 1979–1981, 2nd set Presidents' Ladies/First Ladies Series (Martha) 125.00
TYROLEAN BOY & GIRL* — 8" h.p., BKW (girl - #398, #798; boy - #399, #799), 1962–1965 (Wendy Ann) . .150.00 each
   8" h.p., BK (girl - #798; boy - #799), 1965–1972 . . . . .100.00 each
   8" straight leg (girl - #0798; boy - #0799), 1973, marked "ALEX" . . . . .75.00 each
   8" BKW (Maggie Mixup) . . . . .165.00 each

* BECAME AUSTRIA IN 1974.

·············· PLEASE READ "WHAT IS A PRICE GUIDE?" FOR ADDITIONAL INFORMATION ···············

UGLY STEPSISTER — 10", h.p., #13340, 1997 – 1998, Cinderella series 85.00
ULTIMATE ANGEL — 21", #10770, 1999, blue silk and lace gown 550.00
U.F.D.C. SAILOR BOY — 1990 (see Special Events/Exclusives)
U.S.A. — 8" h.p., #536, 1993–1994 (#110536) (also see Neiman-Marcus trunk set, 1994) 75.00
UNCLE SAM — 8", #10353, 1995 only (Wendy) 70.00
    8", h.p., #24170, 1999, astronaut costume 85.00
UNITED STATES — 8" h.p., #559, straight leg, 1974–1975, marked "Alex" 75.00
    8" #559 Alex. mold, misspelled "Untied States" 100.00
    Straight leg, #559, 1976–1987, marked "Alexander" 65.00
    #559, #516, 1988–1992 (Maggie face) 60.00
    8", #11562, 1996, Statue of Liberty costume, #24000, 1997 – 1998 . . . . .80.00
UNITED STATES ARMED FORCES SET — 4 dolls, 5 flags, and flag stand .350.00
UNITED STATES AIR FORCE — 8", #12000, 1998 (Wendy), uniform and flag 90.00
UNITED STATES ARMY — 8", #12010, 1998 (Wendy) 90.00
UNITED STATES MARINES — 8", #12030, 1998 (Wendy) 90.00
UNITED STATES NAVY — 8", #12020, 1998 (Wendy) 90.00
UNION OFFICER — 12", #634, 1990–1991, Scarlett Series (Nancy Drew) 85.00
    SOLDIER — 8", #634, 1991 only, Scarlett Series 125.00

United States, 8", 1974 – 1987 (Wendy). Notice the long curls on the left.

V

PLEASE READ "WHAT IS A PRICE GUIDE?" FOR ADDITIONAL INFORMATION

VALENTINE — (see Lady Valentine & Lord Valentine)

VAN BUREN, ANGELICA — 1979–1981, 2nd set Presidents' Ladies/First Ladies Series (Louisa) 125.00

VELVET PARTY DRESS — 8", h.p., #389, 1957 only, very rare . . . . .2,000.00 up

VERMONT MAID — 8" (see Enchanted Doll House under Special Events/Exclusives)

VICTORIA — 21" compo., 1939, 1941, 1945–1946 (also see **FLAVIA**) (Wendy Ann) . . . . .2,000.00 up

  20" h.p., 1954 only, Me & My Shadow Series (Cissy) . . . . .1,950.00 up

  14" h.p., 1950–1951 (Margaret) 875.00

  18" h.p., 1954 only, Me & My Shadow Series, slate blue gown (Maggie) . . . . .1,800.00 up

  8" h.p., #0030C, 1954 only, matches 18" doll (Wendy Ann) . . . . .1,100.00 up

  14" baby, 1975–1988, 1990–1997 . . . . .95.00

  18" baby, 1966 only 75.00

  18" reintroduced, 1991–1993, 1997 . . . . .65.00–125.00

  20" baby, 1967–1989 . . . . .100.00

  20" 1986 only, in dress/jacket/bonnet 100.00

  18", vinyl, 1998, velour romper, #29420 white, #29423 African American 110.00

VICTORIAN — 18" h.p., 1953 only, blue taffeta/black velvet gown, Glamour Girl Series (Margaret) . . . .1,500.00 up

VICTORIAN BRIDE — 10", #1148, #1118, 1992 only, Portrette 110.00

  10", blue satin and lace gown 135.00

VICTORIAN BRIDE — (see **DEBRA**)

VICTORIAN CATHERINE — 16", #90010, porcelain, elaborate gown 300.00

VICTORIAN CHRISTMAS — 8", #19970, red velvet and lace 95.00

VICTORIAN SKATER — 10", #1155, 1993–1994, Portrette, red/gold/black outfit (Cissette) 175.00

VIETNAM — 8" h.p., #788, 1968–1969 (Wendy Ann) 275.00

  #788, 1968–1969 (Maggie Mixup) 300.00

  8", #505, reintroduced in 1990–1991 (Maggie) 75.00

VIOLET — (see Sweet Violet)

VIOLET — (Nutcracker Ballerina) 10" Portrette, 1994 only 80.00

VIOLETTA — 10", #1116, 1987–1988, all deep blue (Cissette) 70.00

VIRGO — 8", #21380, pink pleated outfit, gold helmet 90.00

••••••••••••••• PLEASE READ "WHAT IS A PRICE GUIDE?" FOR ADDITIONAL INFORMATION •••••••••••••••

W.A.A.C. (ARMY) — 14" compo., 1943–1944 (Wendy Ann) . . . . .750.00 up
W.A.A.F. (AIR FORCE) — 14" compo., 1943–1944 (Wendy Ann) . . . . .750.00 up
W.A.V.E. (NAVY) — 14" compo., 1943–1944 (Wendy Ann) . . . . .750.00 up
WALTZ — 16", 1999, pink gown trimmed in maribou 190.00
WALTZING — 8" h.p., #476, 1955 only (Wendy Ann) . . . . .725.00 up
WANT — 8", #18406, 1996, Dickens (see Ghost of Christmas Present) (sold as set)
WASHINGTON, MARTHA — 1976–1978, 1st set Presidents' Ladies/First Ladies Series (Martha) 250.00
WATCHFUL GUARDIAN ANGEL — 10", #10740, 1998–1999, blue, white outfit 190.00
WATCHFUL GUARDIAN ANGEL SET — 3 dolls, bridge, gift card 395.00
WEEPING PRINCESS — 8", #11104, 1995 only, International Folk Tales (Maggie) 65.00
WELCOME HOME–DESERT STORM — 8", 1991 only, mid-year introduction, boy or girl soldier, black or white . .55.00
WENDY — 8", 1989, first doll offered to club members only (see M.A.D.C. under Special Events/Exclusives)

W.A.A.C., 14", composition (Wendy Ann). Made from 1943 – 1944. Tagged: "W.A.A.C./Madame Alexander."

WENDY ANGEL — 8" h.p., #404, 1954 (Wendy Ann) . . . . . . .850.00 up
WENDY BALLERINA — 8", (Wendy) 1999, pink trim on
    white lace tutu 80.00
WENDY (FROM PETER PAN) — 15" h.p., 1953 only
    (Margaret) . . . . .550.00 up
    14" plastic/vinyl, #1415, 1969 only (Mary Ann) 275.00
    8", #466 in 1991 to 1993; #140466 in 1994;
    Storyland Series, pom-poms on slippers (Peter Pan) 80.00
WENDY CHEERLEADER — 8", #16500, 1998, pleated skirt,
    red sweater 85.00
WENDY ELF — 8", #12818, 1995, Christmas Series 70.00
WENDY SHOPS FAO —
    (see FAO Schwarz under Special Events/Exclusives)
WENDY LOVES BEING LOVED — 8", 1992–1993 only,
    doll and wardrobe 150.00
BEING JUST LIKE MOMMY — 8", #801, 1993,
    has baby carriage #120801, 1994 . . . . .125.00
THE COUNTRY FAIR — 8", #802, 1993, has cow
    #120802, 1994 . . . . .85.00
SUMMER BOX SET — #805-1993, #120805–1994;
WINTER BOX SET #120810–1994.
    Boxed doll and wardrobe 90.00
LEARNING TO SEW — 8", #120809, 1994,
    in wicker case 125.00
HER FIRST DAY AT SCHOOL — 8", #120806,
    1994–1995 . . . . .75.00
BEING PROM QUEEN — #120808, 1994 . . . . .65.00
HER SUNDAY BEST — 8", #120807, 1994–1995 . . . . .85.00
HER SUNDRESS — #120804, 1994 . . . . .60.00
GOES TO THE CIRCUS — 8", #12819, 1996
    (Wendy Ann) 65.00
WENDY LEARNS HER ABC'S —
    (see ABC Unlimited Productions under Special Events/Exclusives)
WENDY MAKES IT SPECIAL — 8", #31050, 1997–1998,
    pink satin dress 80.00
WENDY SALUTES THE OLYMPICS — 8", #86005, 1996,
    Olympic Medal 150.00

WENDY TAP DANCER — 8", h.p., #13930, 1998, white jacket, gold tap pants 95.00
WENDY THE GARDENER — 8", #31400, 1998–1999, sunflower outfit, watering can, sunflowers 90.00
WENDY VISITS WORLD FAIR —(see Shirley's Doll House under Special Events/Exclusives)
WENDY WORKS CONSTRUCTION — 8", #31420, 1998–1999, includes tools and toolbox 90.00
WENDY'S SPECIAL CHEER — 8", #16500, 1998–1999, cheerleading outfit 80.00
WENDY ANN — 11–15" compo., 1935–1948 . . . . .325.00–575.00
    9" compo., 1936–1940, painted eyes 350.00
    14", 1938–1939, in riding habit, molded hair or wig 400.00
    14", any year, swivel waist, molded hair or wig 425.00
    17–21" compo., 1938–1944 . . . . .550.00–950.00
    14½–17" h.p., 1948–1949 . . . . .600.00–850.00
    16–22" h.p., 1948–1950 . . . . .675.00–975.00
    20" h.p., 1956 (Cissy) 600.00
    23–25" h.p., 1949 . . . . .850.00
    8", #79516, 1995, 100th anniversary, wearing dress, coat, and bonnet, limited production 125.00
WENDY BRIDE — 14–22" compo., 1944–1945 (Wendy Ann) 325.00–500.00
    15–18" h.p., 1951 (Margaret) 600.00–875.00
    20" h.p., 1956 (Cissy) . . . . .650.00 up
    8" h.p., SLW, #475, 1955 (Wendy Ann) 475.00
WENDY KIN BABY — 8", one-piece vinyl body with hard plastic Little Genius head, 1954 . . . . .375.00
WENDY'S DOLLHOUSE TRUNK SET — 8", #12820, 1996 . . . . .225.00
WHITE CHRISTMAS — 10", #10105, 1995 only, Christmas Series 85.00
WHITE CHRISTMA PAIR — 10", #15380, Betty and Bob from the movie 210.00
WHITE IRIS — 10", #22540, white lace and roses 140.00
WHITE KING — 8", h.p., #13020, 1997 – 1998, white suit, cape 100.00
WHITE RABBIT — 14–17", cloth/felt, 1940s 500.00–750.00
    8", #14509, 1995, Alice In Wonderland Series 85.00
    8", #14616, 1996, white rabbit in court 65.00
WICKED STEPMOTHER — 21", #50002, 1996, limited edition 310.00

Wendy Kin Baby, 8", 1954, one piece vinyl body, hard plastic Little Genius head.

WICKED WITCH OF THE WEST — 10", #13270, 1997–1999, (Cissette), black witch costume 105.00
WILSON, EDITH — 1988, 5th set Presidents' Ladies/First Ladies Series (Mary Ann) 125.00
WILSON, ELLEN — 1988, 5th set Presidents' Ladies/First Ladies Series (Louisa) 125.00
WINGED MONKEY — 8" h.p. (Maggie) #140501, 1994 only 275.00
WINNIE WALKER — 15" h.p., 1953 only (Cissy) 275.00
    18–25" 350.00–550.00
    1953–1954, in trunk/trousseau . . . . .850.00 up
WINTER — 14", 1993, Changing Seasons, doll and four outfits 150.00
WINTER FUN SKATER — 8", #10357, 1995, Christmas Series 65.00
WINTER SPORTS — 1991 (see Shirley's Doll House under Special Events/Exclusives)
WINTER WONDERLAND (NASHVILLE SKATER #1) —
    1991–1992 (see Collectors United under Special Events/Exclusives)
WINTER WONDERLAND — 10", #19990, 1999, white satin, fur, jewels 120.00
WINTERTIME — (see M.A.D.C. under Special Events/Exclusives)
WITCH — 8", #322, 1992–1993, Americana Series 75.00
WITH LOVE — 8", #17003, 1996, pink gown, comes with a heart 75.00
    8", #17001, 1996, same as above except African American 75.00
WITCH/HALLOWEEN — (see Collectors United under Special Events/Exclusives)
WITHERS, JANE — 12–13½" compo., 1937, has closed mouth . . . . .1,000.00 up
    15–17", 1937–1939 . . . . .850.00–1,300.00
    17" cloth body, 1939 . . . . .1,500.00
    18–19", 1937–1939 . . . . .1,300.00
    19–20", closed mouth . . . . .1,400.00 up
    20–21", 1937 . . . . .1,600.00 up
WIZARD OF OZ — 8", mid-year special (see Alexander Doll Co. Specials & Exclusives)
    8", #13281, plaid pants, green tailcoat, 1998–1999 . . . . .95.00
    8", with state fair balloon, #13280, with wizard, 1998–1999 . . . . .150.00
1860s WOMEN — 10" h.p., 1990 (see Spiegel's under Special Events/Exclusives) (Beth) 125.00
WYNKIN — (see Dutch Lullaby)

Y

················ PLEASE READ "WHAT IS A PRICE GUIDE?" FOR ADDITIONAL INFORMATION ···················

YOLANDA — 12", 1965 only (Brenda Starr) 375.00
YUGOSLAVIA — 8" h.p., BK, #789, 1968–1972 (Wendy) 90.00
    8" straight leg, #0789, #589, 1973–1975, marked "Alex" 65.00
    8" straight leg, #589, 1976–1986, marked "Alexander" 60.00
    8", 1987 (see Collectors United under Special Events/Exclusives)
YULETIDE ANGEL — (see Tree Toppers)

Z

················ PLEASE READ "WHAT IS A PRICE GUIDE?" FOR ADDITIONAL INFORMATION ···················

ZORINA BALLERINA — 17" compo., 1937–1938, extra makeup,
    must be mint condition (Wendy Ann) .... .1,900.00 up

COLLECTOR BOOKS

Informing Today's Collector

For over two decades we have been keeping collectors informed on trends and values in all fields of antiques and collectibles.

DOLLS, FIGURES & TEDDY BEARS

4707	A Decade of **Barbie** Dolls & Collectibles, 1981–1991, Summers	$19.95
4631	**Barbie** Doll Boom, 1986–1995, Augustyniak	$18.95
2079	**Barbie** Doll Fashion, Volume I, Eames	$24.95
4846	**Barbie** Doll Fashion, Volume II, Eames	$24.95
3957	**Barbie** Exclusives, Rana	$18.95
4632	**Barbie** Exclusives, Book II, Rana	$18.95
4557	**Barbie,** The First 30 Years, Deutsch	$24.95
5252	The **Barbie** Doll Years, 3rd Ed., Olds	$18.95
3810	**Chatty Cathy Dolls**, Lewis	$15.95
1529	Collector's Encyclopedia of **Barbie** Dolls, DeWein	$19.95
4882	Collector's Encyclopedia of **Barbie** Doll Exclusives and More, Augustyniak	$19.95
2211	Collector's Encyclopedia of **Madame Alexander Dolls**, Smith	$24.95
4863	Collector's Encyclopedia of **Vogue Dolls**, Izen/Stover	$29.95
3967	Collector's Guide to **Trolls**, Peterson	$19.95
5253	Story of **Barbie,** 2nd Ed., Westenhouser	$24.95
1513	**Teddy Bears & Steiff** Animals, Mandel	$9.95
1817	**Teddy Bears & Steiff** Animals, 2nd Series, Mandel	$19.95
2084	**Teddy Bears, Annalee's & Steiff** Animals, 3rd Series, Mandel	$19.95
1808	Wonder of **Barbie**, Manos	$9.95
1430	World of **Barbie** Dolls, Manos	$9.95
4880	World of **Raggedy Ann** Collectibles, Avery	$24.95

TOYS, MARBLES & CHRISTMAS COLLECTIBLES

3427	**Advertising Character** Collectibles, Dotz	$17.95
2333	Antique & Collector's **Marbles**, 3rd Ed., Grist	$9.95
4934	**Breyer Animal** Collector's Guide, Identification and Values, Browell	$19.95
4976	**Christmas** Ornaments, Lights & Decorations, Johnson	$24.95
4737	**Christmas** Ornaments, Lights & Decorations, Vol. II, Johnson	$24.95
4739	**Christmas** Ornaments, Lights & Decorations, Vol. III, Johnson	$24.95
4649	Classic Plastic **Model Kits**, Polizzi	$24.95
4559	Collectible **Action Figures,** 2nd Ed., Manos	$17.95
3874	Collectible Coca-Cola Toy **Trucks**, deCourtivron	$24.95
2338	Collector's Encyclopedia of **Disneyana**, Longest, Stern	$24.95
4958	Collector's Guide to **Battery Toys**, Hultzman	$19.95
5038	Collector's Guide to **Diecast Toys & Scale Models,** 2nd Ed., Johnson	$19.95
4651	Collector's Guide to **Tinker Toys,** Strange	$18.95
4566	Collector's Guide to **Tootsietoys,** 2nd Ed., Richter	$19.95
5169	Collector's Guide to **TV Toys** & Memorabilia, 2nd Ed., Davis/Morgan	$24.95
4720	The Golden Age of **Automotive Toys**, 1925–1941, Hutchison/Johnson	$24.95
3436	Grist's Big Book of **Marbles**	$19.95
3970	Grist's Machine-Made & Contemporary **Marbles**, 2nd Ed.	$9.95
5267	**Matchbox** Toys, 1947 to 1998, 3rd Ed., Johnson	$19.95
4871	**McDonald's Collectibles**, Henriques/DuVall	$19.95
1540	**Modern Toys** 1930–1980, Baker	$19.95
3888	**Motorcycle** Toys, Antique & Contemporary, Gentry/Downs	$18.95
5168	Schroeder's Collectible **Toys,** Antique to Modern Price Guide, 5th Ed.	$17.95
1886	Stern's Guide to **Disney** Collectibles	$14.95
2139	Stern's Guide to **Disney** Collectibles, 2nd Series	$14.95
3975	Stern's Guide to **Disney** Collectibles, 3rd Series	$18.95
2028	**Toys**, Antique & Collectible, Longest	$14.95

FURNITURE

1457	American **Oak** Furniture, McNerney	$9.95
3716	American **Oak** Furniture, Book II, McNerney	$12.95
1118	Antique **Oak** Furniture, Hill	$7.95
2271	Collector's Encyclopedia of **American** Furniture, Vol. II, Swedberg	$24.95
3720	Collector's Encyclopedia of **American** Furniture, Vol. III, Swedberg	$24.95
1755	Furniture of the **Depression Era**, Swedberg	$19.95
3906	**Heywood-Wakefield** Modern Furniture, Rouland	$18.95
1885	**Victorian** Furniture, Our American Heritage, McNerney	$9.95
3829	**Victorian** Furniture, Our American Heritage, Book II, McNerney	$9.95

JEWELRY, HATPINS, WATCHES & PURSES

1712	Antique & Collector's **Thimbles** & Accessories, Mathis	$19.95
1748	Antique **Purses,** Revised Second Ed., Holiner	$19.95
1278	Art Nouveau & Art Deco **Jewelry**, Baker	$9.95
4850	Collectible **Costume Jewelry**, Simonds	$24.95
3875	Collecting Antique **Stickpins**, Kerins	$16.95
3722	Collector's Ency. of **Compacts, Carryalls & Face Powder Boxes**, Mueller	$24.95
4854	Collector's Ency. of **Compacts, Carryalls & Face Powder Boxes**, Vol. II	$24.95
4940	**Costume Jewelry**, A Practical Handbook & Value Guide, Rezazadeh	$24.95
1716	Fifty Years of Collectible **Fashion Jewelry**, 1925–1975, Baker	$19.95
1424	**Hatpins** & Hatpin Holders, Baker	$9.95
1181	100 Years of Collectible **Jewelry**, 1850–1950, Baker	$9.95
4729	**Sewing Tools** & Trinkets, Thompson	$24.95
4878	Vintage & Contemporary **Purse Accessories**, Gerson	$24.95
3830	Vintage **Vanity Bags & Purses**, Gerson	$24.95

INDIANS, GUNS, KNIVES, TOOLS, PRIMITIVES

1868	Antique **Tools,** Our American Heritage, McNerney	$9.95
1426	**Arrowheads** & Projectile Points, Hothem	$7.95
4943	Field Guide to **Flint Arrowheads & Knives** of the North American Indian	$9.95
2279	**Indian Artifacts** of the Midwest, Hothem	$14.95
3885	**Indian Artifacts** of the Midwest, Book II, Hothem	$16.95
4870	**Indian Artifacts** of the Midwest, Book III, Hothem	$18.95
5162	Modern **Guns**, Identification & Values, 12th Ed., Quertermous	$12.95
2164	**Primitives**, Our American Heritage, McNerney	$9.95
1759	**Primitives**, Our American Heritage, 2nd Series, McNerney	$14.95
4730	Standard **Knife** Collector's Guide, 3rd Ed., Ritchie & Stewart	$12.95

PAPER COLLECTIBLES & BOOKS

4633	**Big Little Books**, Jacobs	$18.95
4710	Collector's Guide to **Children's Books**, 1850 to 1950, Jones	$18.95
1441	Collector's Guide to **Post Cards**, Wood	$9.95
2081	Guide to Collecting **Cookbooks**, Allen	$14.95
5271	Huxford's **Old Book** Value Guide, 11th Ed.	$19.95
2080	Price Guide to **Cookbooks** & Recipe Leaflets, Dickinson	$9.95
3973	**Sheet Music** Reference & Price Guide, 2nd Ed., Pafik & Guiheen	$19.95
4654	**Victorian Trade Cards,** Historical Reference & Value Guide, Cheadle	$19.95
4733	**Whitman Juvenile Books**, Brown	$17.95

GLASSWARE

4561	Collectible **Drinking Glasses**, Chase & Kelly	$17.95
4642	Collectible **Glass Shoes**, Wheatley	$19.95
4937	Coll. **Glassware from the 40s, 50s & 60s,** 4th Ed., Florence	$19.95
1810	Collector's Encyclopedia of **American Art Glass**, Shuman	$29.95
4938	Collector's Encyclopedia of **Depression Glass,** 13th Ed., Florence	$19.95
1961	Collector's Encyclopedia of **Fry Glassware**, Fry Glass Society	$24.95
1664	Collector's Encyclopedia of **Heisey Glass**, 1925–1938, Bredehoft	$24.95
3905	Collector's Encyclopedia of **Milk Glass**, Newbound	$24.95
4936	Collector's Guide to **Candy Containers**, Dezso/Poirier	$19.95
4564	**Crackle Glass**, Weitman	$19.95
4941	**Crackle Glass**, Book II, Weitman	$19.95
4714	**Czechoslovakian Glass** and Collectibles, Book II, Barta/Rose	$16.95
5158	**Elegant Glassware** of the Depression Era, 8th Ed., Florence	$19.95
1380	Encyclopedia of **Pattern Glass**, McCain	$12.95
3981	Evers' Standard **Cut Glass** Value Guide	$12.95
4659	**Fenton** Art Glass, 1907–1939, Whitmyer	$24.95
3725	**Fostoria,** Pressed, Blown & Hand Molded Shapes, Kerr	$24.95
4719	**Fostoria,** Etched, Carved & Cut Designs, Vol. II, Kerr	$24.95
3883	**Fostoria Stemware**, The Crystal for America, Long & Seate	$24.95
4644	**Imperial Carnival Glass**, Burns	$18.95
3886	**Kitchen Glassware** of the Depression Years, 5th Ed., Florence	$19.95
5156	Pocket Guide to **Depression Glass**, 11th Ed., Florence	$9.95

COLLECTOR BOOKS
Informing Today's Collector

5035	Standard Encyclopedia of **Carnival Glass**, 6th Ed., Edwards/Carwile	$24.95
5036	Standard **Carnival Glass** Price Guide, 11th Ed., Edwards/Carwile	$9.95
5272	Standard Encyclopedia of **Opalescent Glass**, 3rd ed., Edwards	$24.95
5731	**Stemware Identification**, Featuring Cordials with Values, Florence	$24.95
5326	**Very Rare Glassware** of the Depression Years, 3rd Series, Florence	$24.95
5732	**Very Rare Glassware** of the Depression Years, 5th Series, Florence	$24.95
5656	**Westmoreland Glass**, Wilson	$24.95

POTTERY

4927	**ABC Plates & Mugs**, Lindsay	$24.95
4929	**American Art Pottery**, Sigafoose	$24.95
4630	**American Limoges**, Limoges	$24.95
1312	**Blue & White Stoneware**, McNerney	$9.95
1958	So. Potteries **Blue Ridge Dinnerware**, 3rd Ed., Newbound	$14.95
1959	**Blue Willow**, 2nd Ed., Gaston	$14.95
4848	Ceramic **Coin Banks**, Stoddard	$19.95
4851	Collectible **Cups & Saucers**, Harran	$18.95
5709	Collectible **Kay Finch**, Biography, Identification & Values, Martinez/Frick	$18.95
1373	Collector's Encyclopedia of **American Dinnerware**, Cunningham	$24.95
4931	Collector's Encyclopedia of **Bauer Pottery**, Chipman	$24.95
4932	Collector's Encyclopedia of **Blue Ridge Dinnerware**, Vol. II, Newbound	$24.95
4658	Collector's Encyclopedia of **Brush-McCoy Pottery**, Huxford	$24.95
5034	Collector's Encyclopedia of **California Pottery**, 2nd Ed., Chipman	$24.95
2133	Collector's Encyclopedia of **Cookie Jars**, Roerig	$24.95
3723	Collector's Encyclopedia of **Cookie Jars**, Book II, Roerig	$24.95
4939	Collector's Encyclopedia of **Cookie Jars**, Book III, Roerig	$24.95
4638	Collector's Encyclopedia of **Dakota Potteries**, Dommel	$24.95
5040	Collector's Encyclopedia of **Fiesta**, 8th Ed., Huxford	$19.95
4718	Collector's Encyclopedia of **Figural Planters & Vases**, Newbound	$19.95
4961	Collector's Encyclopedia of **Early Noritake**, Alden	$24.95
1439	Collector's Encyclopedia of **Flow Blue China**, Gaston	$19.95
3812	Collector's Encyclopedia of **Flow Blue China**, 2nd Ed., Gaston	$24.95
3813	Collector's Encyclopedia of **Hall China**, 2nd Ed., Whitmyer	$24.95
1431	Collector's Encyclopedia of **Homer Laughlin China**, Jasper	$24.95
1276	Collector's Encyclopedia of **Hull Pottery**, Roberts	$19.95
3962	Collector's Encyclopedia of **Lefton China**, DeLozier	$19.95
5855	Collector's Encyclopedia of **Lefton China**, Book II, DeLozier	$19.95
2210	Collector's Encyclopedia of **Limoges Porcelain**, 2nd Ed., Gaston	$24.95
2334	Collector's Encyclopedia of **Majolica Pottery**, Katz-Marks	$19.95
1358	Collector's Encyclopedia of **McCoy Pottery**, Huxford	$19.95
3963	Collector's Encyclopedia of **Metlox Potteries**, Gibbs Jr.	$24.95
1837	Collector's Encyclopedia of **Nippon Porcelain**, Van Patten	$24.95
2089	Collector's Ency. of **Nippon Porcelain**, 2nd Series, Van Patten	$24.95
1665	Collector's Ency. of **Nippon Porcelain**, 3rd Series, Van Patten	$24.95
4712	Collector's Ency. of **Nippon Porcelain**, 4th Series, Van Patten	$24.95
1447	Collector's Encyclopedia of **Noritake**, Van Patten	$19.95
1037	Collector's Encyclopedia of **Occupied Japan**, 1st Series, Florence	$14.95
1038	Collector's Encyclopedia of **Occupied Japan**, 2nd Series, Florence	$14.95
2088	Collector's Encyclopedia of **Occupied Japan**, 3rd Series, Florence	$14.95
2019	Collector's Encyclopedia of **Occupied Japan**, 4th Series, Florence	$14.95
2335	Collector's Encyclopedia of **Occupied Japan**, 5th Series, Florence	$14.95
4951	Collector's Encyclopedia of **Old Ivory China**, Hillman	$24.95
3964	Collector's Encyclopedia of **Pickard China**, Reed	$24.95
4877	Collector's Encyclopedia of **R.S. Prussia**, 4th Series, Gaston	$24.95
1034	Collector's Encyclopedia of **Roseville Pottery**, Huxford	$19.95
1035	Collector's Encyclopedia of **Roseville Pottery**, 2nd Ed., Huxford	$19.95
4856	Collector's Encyclopedia of **Russel Wright**, 2nd Ed., Kerr	$24.95
5713	Collector's Encyclopedia of **Salt Glaze Stoneware**, Taylor/Lowrance	$24.95
5814	Collector's Encyclopedia of **Van Briggle** Art Pottery, Sasicki	$24.95
5563	Collector's Encyclopedia of **Wall Pockets**, Newbound	$19.95
2111	Collector's Encyclopedia of **Weller Pottery**, Huxford	$29.95
5676	Collector's Guide to **Lu-Ray Pastels**, Meehan	$18.95
2379	Collector's Guide to **Made in Japan** Ceramics, White	$18.95
5646	Collector's Guide to **Made in Japan** Ceramics, Book II, White	$18.95
3439	Collector's Guide to **Shawnee Pottery**, Vanderbilt	$19.95

1425	**Cookie Jars**, Westfall	$9.95
3440	**Cookie Jars**, Book II, Westfall	$19.95
4924	Figural & Novelty **Salt & Pepper Shakers**, 2nd Series, Davern	$24.95
2379	Lehner's Ency. of **U.S. Marks** on Pottery, Porcelain & China	$24.95
4722	**McCoy Pottery**, Collector's Reference & Value Guide, Hanson/Nissen	$19.95
4726	**Red Wing Art Pottery**, 1920s–1960s, Dollen	$19.95
1670	**Red Wing Collectibles**, DePasquale	$9.95
1440	**Red Wing Stoneware**, DePasquale	$9.95
1632	**Salt & Pepper Shakers**, Guarnaccia	$9.95
5091	**Salt & Pepper Shakers** II, Guarnaccia	$18.95
2220	**Salt & Pepper Shakers** III, Guarnaccia	$14.95
3443	**Salt & Pepper Shakers** IV, Guarnaccia	$18.95
3738	**Shawnee Pottery**, Mangus	$24.95
4629	Turn of the Century **American Dinnerware**, 1880s–1920s, Jasper	$24.95
3327	**Watt Pottery** – Identification & Value Guide, Morris	$19.95

OTHER COLLECTIBLES

4704	Antique & Collectible **Buttons**, Wisniewski	$19.95
2269	Antique **Brass & Copper** Collectibles, Gaston	$16.95
1880	Antique **Iron**, McNerney	$9.95
3872	Antique **Tins**, Dodge	$24.95
4845	Antique **Typewriters & Office Collectibles**, Rehr	$19.95
1714	**Black** Collectibles, Gibbs	$19.95
1128	**Bottle** Pricing Guide, 3rd Ed., Cleveland	$7.95
4636	**Celluloid Collectibles**, Dunn	$14.95
3718	Collectible **Aluminum**, Grist	$16.95
4560	Collectible **Cats**, An Identification & Value Guide, Book II, Fyke	$19.95
4852	Collectible **Compact Disc** Price Guide 2, Cooper	$17.95
2018	Collector's Encyclopedia of **Granite Ware**, Greguire	$24.95
3430	Collector's Encyclopedia of **Granite Ware**, Book 2, Greguire	$24.95
4705	Collector's Guide to **Antique Radios**, 4th Ed., Bunis	$18.95
3880	Collector's Guide to **Cigarette Lighters**, Flanagan	$17.95
4637	Collector's Guide to **Cigarette Lighters**, Book II, Flanagan	$17.95
4942	Collector's Guide to **Don Winton Designs**, Ellis	$19.95
3966	Collector's Guide to **Inkwells**, Identification & Values, Badders	$18.95
4947	Collector's Guide to **Inkwells**, Book II, Badders	$19.95
4948	Collector's Guide to **Letter Openers**, Grist	$19.95
4862	Collector's Guide to **Toasters & Accessories**, Greguire	$19.95
4652	Collector's Guide to **Transistor Radios**, 2nd Ed., Bunis	$16.95
4864	Collector's Guide to **Wallace Nutting Pictures**, Ivankovich	$18.95
1629	**Doorstops**, Identification & Values, Bertoia	$9.95
4567	Figural **Napkin Rings**, Gottschalk & Whitson	$18.95
4717	Figural **Nodders**, Includes Bobbin' Heads and Swayers, Irtz	$19.95
3968	**Fishing Lure** Collectibles, Murphy/Edmisten	$24.95
5259	**Flea Market Trader**, 12th Ed., Huxford	$9.95
4944	**Flue Covers**, Collector's Value Guide, Meckley	$12.95
4945	**G-Men and FBI Toys** and Collectibles, Whitworth	$18.95
5263	**Garage Sale & Flea Market Annual**, 7th Ed.	$19.95
3819	**General Store Collectibles**, Wilson	$24.95
5159	Huxford's Collectible **Advertising**, 4th Ed.	$24.95
2216	**Kitchen Antiques**, 1790–1940, McNerney	$14.95
4950	The **Lone Ranger**, Collector's Reference & Value Guide, Felbinger	$18.95
2026	**Railroad** Collectibles, 4th Ed., Baker	$14.95
5167	**Schroeder's Antiques Price Guide**, 17th Ed., Huxford	$12.95
5007	**Silverplated Flatware**, Revised 4th Edition, Hagan	$18.95
1922	Standard **Old Bottle** Price Guide, Sellari	$14.95
5154	Summers' Guide to **Coca-Cola**, 2nd Ed.	$19.95
4952	Summers' Pocket Guide to **Coca-Cola** Identifications	$9.95
3892	**Toy & Miniature Sewing Machines**, Thomas	$18.95
4876	**Toy & Miniature Sewing Machines**, Book II, Thomas	$24.95
5144	Value Guide to **Advertising Memorabilia**, 2nd Ed., Summers	$19.95
3977	Value Guide to **Gas Station** Memorabilia, Summers & Priddy	$24.95
4877	Vintage **Bar Ware**, Visakay	$24.95
4935	The W.F. Cody **Buffalo Bill** Collector's Guide with Values	$24.95
5281	**Wanted to Buy**, 7th Edition	$9.95

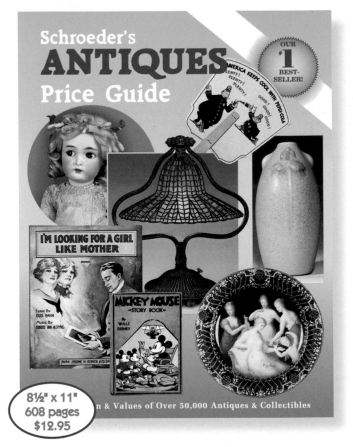